Commendations for
From Strangers to Neighbours

'. . . How to bridge the gaps between the Church and the world . . .'

Rev Dr Rob Frost
(National Evangelist, Methodist Church)

'. . . This highly informative book . . .'
Gerald Coates (Pioneer Church leader)

'Deeply challenging, superbly researched, well-written and full of practical examples of how Christians can make a real difference to poverty and injustice.'
Dr Patrick Dixon (House Church leader)

'. . . The product of numerous reflections on behalf of the poor, disenfranchised and marginalised . . .'
Rev Joel Edwards
(General Director, Evangelical Alliance)

'. . . Followers of Jesus reflect and act – they are "community-makers" . . .'

Ray Bakke
(Director, International Urban Associates, USA)

'. . . Challenging Christians to put their faith into action . . . graphic and accessible . . . a prophetic and practical call . . .'

Angela Sarkis
(Chief Executive, Church Urban Fund)

'. . . How to apply lessons from around the world on our own doorstep . . .'

Rev Steve Chalke
(National Director, Oasis Trust)

'. . . A timely and significant contribution . . . authenticated from the authors' own experiences . . . contemporary models to challenge, inspire and probably frighten us . . .'

Roger Forster
(Ichthus Christian Fellowship leader)

From Strangers to Neighbours

How You Can Make the Difference in Your Community

David Evans and Mike Fearon

Hodder & Stoughton

LONDON SYDNEY AUCKLAND

British Library Cataloguing in Publication Data
A record for this book is available from the British Library

ISBN 0 340 69455 6

Typeset by Avon Dataset Ltd, Bidford-on-Avon, Warks

Printed and bound in Great Britain by
Clays Ltd St Ives plc, Bungay, Suffolk

Hodder and Stoughton
A division of Hodder Headline PLC
338 Euston Road
London NW1 3BH

Contents

Foreword

From Strangers to Neighbours is a book much needed in our churches today and I hope that it will be widely read.

It spells out the very clear duty of Christians to love our neighbours. It tells us who those neighbours are, why they do not come to church for help and the kind of help we can give. It points out that if we deal with the needs which they feel most acutely and they come to see us as true friends as well as neighbours, they are more likely to talk to us about the more important needs which they do not yet feel.

But the book is quite clear that our Lord's care was not simply a means of proselytising. As many he healed turned away from him and only a few stayed to listen, so it will be with us. God's love is indivisible and we must love as unconditionally as he does.

Yet the book is much more than a lecture on caring. It draws on the experience of Tear Fund across the world, and is full of all kinds of characters and the stories about them. It is a 'good read' and I commend it most warmly!

Sir Fred Catherwood

Acknowledgments

We are grateful to the following who agreed to be interviewed specifically for this book: David Ainge, Doug Balfour, Jennie Collins, David Connolly, Clive Furness, Rob Gallagher, Ram Gidoomal, Adrian Hawkes, Bob Holman, Alan Horne, Terry Jones, Barry Lock, John Matthews, Martin Neil, René Padilla, Chris Peacock, Greg Smith, Bev Thomas, Robin Thompson, Keith Tondeur, and Ian Wallace.

The following were interviewed in other contexts: Dave Andrews, Sonny Arguinzoni, Steve Chalke, Graham Cray, Nicky Cruz, Roger Forster, Russell Grubb, John Kirkby, Vishal Mangalwadi, Jaisankar Sarma, and Jim Wallis.

We are grateful for the help given by Gordon Barley, Dewi Hughes, Justin McKenzie, Anna Pearson, Annabel Robson and Mike Webb *in the preparation of the final text. Pontius' Puddle appears courtesy of* Joel Kauffmann. *Cover photography by* Richard Hanson, Mike Webb and Greenleaf. *Apologies to* Enid Blyton, Chris Carter, C. S. Lewis and Gene Roddenberry. *Special thanks to Sir Fred Catherwood.*

Comments about this book can be e-mailed to 106251.1671@ compuserve.com

Prologue

What *is* a Christian? What function do they have? If you were to ask Wormwood, the junior demon from C. S. Lewis's *Screwtape Letters*, he might give you a very jaundiced view:

'. . . Their function is to live happy and contented lives, keeping themselves to themselves, and having nothing whatsoever to do with poorer members of the community. Good Hades, you don't want to go mixing with the riff-raff! If you're not careful, some of them might start coming to your church and lowering the tone of the place. No, you don't want to let that happen.

'Dear reader, you've made a terrible mistake purchasing this book,' Wormwood might add. 'You won't like it, you know. Those dreadful people, David Evans and Mike Fearon, will try to run you ragged with all their outlandish notions. You'd be much better throwing the book in the bin and settling down in front of the TV to "chill out" like a couch potato. Or pour yourself a stiff drink, have a lovely lie in the bath, and get an early night. Yes, that sounds like a wonderful lifestyle for an intelligent Christian to follow. And you are such a lovely person, but you don't want to spoil it by getting too much religion, you know.'

'No Win' Situation?

Others might argue that the fundamental purpose of being a Christian is to make *more* Christians. Like the miniature robots of nano-technology, they stealthily transform the most unlikely of raw material into shiny-haloed clones, tracts in hand, ready to go out and multiply. But what is the purpose of all these conversion machines?

'To witness to the eternal truths of the Christian faith, and to win others to accept those beliefs,' says the theologian. 'There are three basic truths. First, that God made the good earth, with people as the pinnacle of the created order. Second, that men and women fell from grace through disobedient interference with the created order – tasting the forbidden fruit. Third, God rectified the situation – by being born as a perfect person, living a blameless life, and dying an atoning death for the sins of the first Man, and his descendants.' In this view, the non-Christian is invited to partake of the benefits of Christ's death, through confession, repentance, and acceptance of Christ as Lord and Saviour.

Though admirable in theory, the model's practical execution is tricky – largely because considerable time is required to develop personal relationships in which to share this belief system. It's not a good idea to be the cause of a guilt trip by making people feel that they are a cross between Adolf Hitler and Genghis Khan, through stressing their original sin before you've even begun to get to know them properly!

Some argue that Christians are still sometimes prone to over-simplification, concerned only with a person's spiritual needs, to the exclusion of the mental, emotional and physical. The Church's mission is more than stuffing people into a religious sausage machine and churning out an unending chain of spiritual bangers! Christianity is sometimes seen as a manufacturing industry – making new Christians. For some other churchmen, it is (if you'll excuse the pun) a service industry – a *Sunday* service industry . . .

Anglo-Catholic churchmanship focuses on tradition and a corporate view of outreach. They tend to be very concerned with social issues, but priests will also hold communion by proxy for the non-Christian parishioners. The liberals have an all-embracing view of ministry that has minimal boundaries. For instance, Jesus is only one way to God, there are many others.

You just can't win! It seems that, whatever you believe and however you act, someone somewhere is not going to like you for it! Yet it *is* possible to have the best of all worlds; indeed, it is *essential* that God's people have lives that are well balanced in the physical, emotional, mental *and* spiritual spheres. It is an uncomfortable experience to be out of balance. God wants spiritual fruit, not religious nuts!

It's not simply those who have yet to come to Christ who are prone to guilt trips. Many believers have guilt complexes because they are unable to make their spiritual life interlace with their everyday working world, and because they feel they should be 'doing more'. They believe their faith should inspire their actions, and their actions validate their faith, but it never seems to happen. Because they feel so *guilty* about Christian mission, and so *fearful* of being an inadequate and ineffectual Christian, they are afraid to take risks with God. They are petrified that any activity they contemplate may be the wrong move. So, instead of taking action, they take out their cheque book; or instead of giving their time, they give cash.

But this fiscal approach to the poor denies a Christian the opportunity to become *spiritually wealthy* through sharing in Christ's suffering and glorification. Many Christians want the glory without the pain – the resurrection without the cross – but the cup of suffering is extended to all who own Christ's name and who seek to follow in his sandal prints. Guilt is a poor substitute for motivation. Christ forgives and frees his followers from guilt. The God of the Bible is not a small, parochial deity; he is Lord of heaven and earth, and through Christ he commands his people: 'Go and make disciples of all nations' (Matt. 28:19).

Mission Impossible?

Concern about evangelism is frequently the Christian's chief guilt syndrome – it's something we really enjoy having a good fret about! If each of Britain's one million evangelical Christians brought one other person to God every month, discipling that person so that they too made a new Christian every month, then the whole country would be converted inside six months. Well, it's not going to happen! If it was, it would have happened before now. Too often, evangelism is something that Christians do *to* people, instead of *with* them. It is not an honest and genuine sharing, but a neurosis fuelled by an overactive sense of contrition. Church of Scotland minister John Matthews says:

> Churches are throwing away the long sermons, the intercessions and the theologically-weighty hymns, in favour of short snappy talks, strumming guitars and syncopated rhythms. There is nothing necessarily wrong with any of that, but it has not been conspicuously successful in attracting thousands of new people into each church. The people for whom the service has been made shallow and glib still don't come, and perhaps the baby has gone down the plughole with the bathwater. Mature Christians for whom the lengthy sermons and wide variety of worship styles were meaningful are finding themselves unfed.
>
> People often want a quiet time in church, to 'set them up' for the week ahead. They don't want too many newcomers who might upset the routine. They certainly don't want to get involved in mission.

As for community, keep it outside where it belongs! They want to love God, but their neighbours are an altogether different proposition. They may ask God to increase their numbers, but if he did, most of the worshippers might get a bit of a fright! Their prayer might be, 'Lord, send another fifty people into our congregation, but please make sure that they are all just like me.'

It would be wonderful if the Church could produce massive

conversions, simply through holding big rallies and inviting a noted speaker who would do all the work. But it's not that simple. It doesn't work! It's difficult to get people to come to a rally – even when someone like Dr Billy Graham is speaking – and all too often, many of the converts drift away pretty soon afterwards.

It's hardly surprising that modern Westerners are so reluctant to commit to something as nebulous as a long-term relationship with God when they won't even commit to long-term relationships *with each other*. It has become society's norm for people to live together in often transient relationships (serial monogamy) without bothering to go off to church and get 'hitched' – perhaps because they're frightened that the minister may be vocal in disapproving of sex before marriage. Thirty-five per cent of children born in Britain are now conceived outside of wedlock. Many people of today are allergic to commitment in any form.

Indifference is not simply confined to the developed world. Black South African Caesar Molebatsi lost a leg when he was knocked off his bike by a white driver when he was fifteen. The driver came back to look at him, threw a blanket over him, but didn't bother to take Caesar to a hospital. He overcame his bitterness, through a personal encounter with Jesus Christ, and went on to lead Youth Alive Ministries in Soweto. YAM gives Bible teaching, but it also runs a feeding and relief programme, an educational support programme, and a small-business development scheme. If God could bring something good out of the wreckage of Caesar's life, then we should not lose hope. But it's going to be an uphill struggle.

For pity's sake, the Church needs to stop and listen, to reflect and to rethink its method and style of communications. Actions speak louder than words and, until church members *demonstrate* their faith through the compassionate way they relate to others in their local community, their words will simply be blown away by the hurricane force of people's preconceptions of 'churchianity' and their poor opinion of a faith that seems all 'pie in the sky'.

Authentic Christianity

This brings us back to the original question: *What is a Christian?*

Instead of considering the matter in terms of 'what activities define a Christian', or arguing the toss between evangelism and social action, it is perhaps best to look at what it means *relationally*. In an evangelistic setting, it's perhaps best to start with God as creator and then leave it there for the moment, leaving a better chance of developing a relationship in which the basic nature of people can be explored at a later date.

Becoming a Christian essentially means *entering a relationship with God*. It is a father–child relationship. Initially the new-born child is helpless and totally dependent upon the divine parent, then freedom of thought and action follow, within determined but evolving parameters. Eventually the Christian comes to share fully in God's work as the relationship becomes a partnership: 'God and son', or 'God and daughter'. But God always comes first, and we never lose the need for our loving father to be with us every step of the way.

We were all one family, from the very beginning. We are *all* God's children – Christian and non-Christian alike – because we are all created in his image, but some have 'got the hang of it' more than others. *Some have accepted God's parenthood while others haven't!* Only through Christ are we able to understand our basic nature – what it means to be God's children – because Christ is the role model, God's *perfect* child. In the Bible we see him living out a radical theology that is truly *incarnational*, not static but growing and developing as it is lived out in practice.

Here there is much with which even a non-Christian will agree. The notion that all humanity is a universal brotherhood, because we are all God's children, is a brilliant starting point for evangelism and social action alike. We are to *love* one another as though we were all literally brothers and sisters, and that simple statement is theologically very profound. As the apostle Paul put it: 'If I have the gift of prophecy and can fathom all mysteries and all knowledge, and I have a faith that can move mountains, but have not love, I am nothing' (1 Cor. 13:2). Paul's words have their echo in the music and literature of every generation. As the pinnacle of the European symphonic tradition, Beethoven set Schiller's *Ode to Joy* to music in the final movement of his awesome Ninth Symphony: 'All mankind become brothers, where thy gentle wing tarries . . . Brothers! Beyond the canopy of stars a loving father must live.' A hundred and forty-two years later, the Beatles sang 'All You Need Is Love'; indeed, 'love' is the most used word in popular song titles. Christ said, 'Love your neighbour *as yourself*' (Luke 10:27). 'Do to others as you would have them do to you,' is a creed to which the whole world will willingly say 'Amen!'

In answer to the question, 'Who is my neighbour?' Jesus told the parable of the Good Samaritan, defining the meaning of 'neighbour' in the broadest possible terms; it was not the priest or the Levite who best characterised the neighbourly spirit, but a Samaritan. We are perhaps intended to understand the word 'neighbour' as synonymous with 'community' or 'society', but the specific example that Christ gives – a Samaritan – is someone whom the orthodox Jews of Jesus's day regarded as 'beyond the pale'. A Samaritan was a kind of 'bogus Jew', a person of foreign descent who lived on territory that had traditionally belonged to the Jewish people. They mimicked Jewish traditions, and desperately wanted to be regarded as Jewish, but the Jews regarded them only as counterfeits and outsiders: 'Not our kind, mate!' So those that Christ *specifically* says we are to love as much as we love ourselves are *those who have been rejected and spurned by normal society!* They are an underclass, deeply in need of love and affection.

There is so much ambiguous use of the words 'community', 'society' and 'neighbourhood' in academic texts these days that some people consider that 'family' might be a better word. The Family of Man, or all humanity, is intended by God to be one another's keeper. This notion of universal love was popular with the hippies of the 1960s, and events like Live Aid in 1985 made the world think again that concepts like 'peace, love and understanding' were maybe not so funny after all. The 1990s saw a revival of these ideals, particularly amongst young people in the dance culture. In the words of an old Les Paul song, 'The world is waiting for the sunrise,' and the mood of society is currently one of openness to change. There is a grassroots willingness for people to help one another; to 'feed the world' and make it a better place.

Evangelism needs to start where people are actually 'at'. Everyday people are generally very willing to help with 'good works', yet many Christians take the view that such people should be disenfranchised from taking part in the Church's ministry until such time as they have learned the Four Spiritual Laws; memorised the Ten Commandments; had hands laid upon them by a bishop; or entered into church membership. Up in heaven, Christ shakes his head, and wonders how well-intentioned people have managed to get his teaching quite so wrong.

The Way Ahead

Piety without practice is impotent, according to Greg Smith, a community development worker based in East London:

> As I continue to read the Bible I am more and more convinced that God thinks and feels the same way, and that he is already doing something to heal the whole created order. The Church is not an institution, but the organic body of Christ, subject to both infirmity and growth. To achieve the latter, it needs to commit itself to making disciples, with a spirit of servanthood. Self-examination, confession and repentance are all on the menu.

Vision and boldness will follow as we get on our hermeneutical cycles and become pedlars of the Gospel!

There are three main areas where this book will provide fresh insights into an area which has been the topic of much recent interest and discussion.

First, Tear Fund – the sponsor of this book – has vast experience working with overseas partners, and community development has been one of the main areas it has supported for many years. This book will show how Christian community development approaches which are well tried overseas can be applied in urban areas of the developed world. The clear distinction between *welfare*-oriented approaches and more *developmental* approaches will be provided, and insight will be given into the West's essentially counter-productive welfare mindset.

Second, we are aware that the time-honoured vocabulary of 'evangelism' and 'social action' often causes problems for local churches when they suggest an 'either-or' approach. The following pages show how using the term 'Christian community development' effectively incorporates both elements, and prevents an unhelpful separation in the minds of those Christians who want to make a real difference locally. When dignity and respect are given to people who are trapped by circumstances, change becomes possible. Showing dignity and respect are *spiritual* issues as much as *emotional* and *social* issues.

Third, the book will show from first-hand practical experience how *experienced-based learning* changes people's attitudes more effectively than approaches which rely more on preaching or teaching from the front. The model of Jesus's training style with the disciples was essentially *experience-based*, using action and reflection to put across the values of the Kingdom of God.

It is not just those outside the Church who need to change and adapt. Christians, too, need to develop their faith to tackle the challenges of a new millennium. 'The poor evangelise the Church,' say many South American theologians, and the transformation is excruciatingly painful. The transformation can begin here, right now, through reading this book. If you picked it up because you thought it might be a pleasant read, you'd better go and get your money back! You're going to be deeply challenged by some of the people you will meet in the following pages. Your most cherished sacred cows are likely to end up as the filling in a 'Big Mac'.

New birth is painful, as any mother will tell you.

1

Community

On the bridge of the U.S.S. *Enterprise*, Captain James T. Kirk adjusts his toupee and turns, with an object in his hand, to his Vulcan first officer: 'Clearly a twentieth-century artefact, Mr Spock.'

'Aye, captain, an old-style paperback book entitled *From Strangers to Neighbours*, on the subject of community development.'

'Weren't there a lot of other texts published on the same subject, Spock? They must all be similar,' says Kirk, his square jaw jutting manfully.

'Illogical, Captain,' replies the Vulcan, twitching his pointed ears. 'This book reflected a very new approach to social issues in the context of Christian mission.'

'It's *evangelism*, Jim, but not as we know it!' chips in Dr 'Bones' McCoy. 'Quite ground-breaking. It seems that the Christians of that era needed a photon torpedo up their . . .'

'Thank you, Bones.'

A century or two later, on a different U.S.S. *Enterprise*, Captain Jean-Luc Picard turns to his own first officer. 'Very moving,' he says, putting the book down to wipe a tear from his eye.

'Late twentieth-century Earth was a cauldron of despair,' nods Commander William Riker, reaching for another Kleenex tissue. 'Vision and compassion were needed to achieve change.'

Whereas Jim Kirk, in the original *Star Trek* television series, was prone to deal with his adversaries by firing his phasers and photon torpedoes at the enemy's ship – or on occasions resorting to a swift punch on the jaw to put the baddies in their place – Jean-Luc Picard in *Star Trek: The Next Generation*, made twenty years later, was more likely to invite his foes for a chat over a cup of Earl Grey: 'It wasn't very nice destroying that planet with its twenty billion inhabitants, you know. Tut tut! You really should try to control these aggressive tendencies. Perhaps you should make an appointment to see our ship's counsellor . . .'

The differences have less to do with the imagined changes in society over the 150 years or so that separate the eras in which the two programmes are set, so much as changes in the real world during the two decades between the filming of the two series. Captain Kirk's original TV series was concurrent with the Vietnam war, in which the USA's bullish gunboat mentality sought to preserve the free world from, respectively, the 'yellow peril' and 'the Reds', where 'the only good commie is a commie who's dead, and don't forget it, mister!' James T. Kirk was John Wayne in tights, boldly going where no man had gone before, meeting representatives of strange and wonderful races – and then slaughtering them.

Jean-Luc's commitment to the peaceful resolution of conflicts was a reaction to the selfishness and greed of the 1980s, when money ruled and rampant drug abuse led to rich stockbrokers and poor street junkies alike turning to crack cocaine for illicit thrills, getting higher than Mr Spock without the need for a starship. In American culture where people tend to visit their psychiatrist more frequently than their church minister, the psycho-analysis, interpersonal dynamics and self-improvement of twenty-fourth century society seemed quite homely. An empathic counsellor was obviously essential to the emotional well-being of any ship's crew.

A person 'beaming down' into any major city in the real 1980s would have found a very different situation from someone standing in the same place twenty years earlier. Changing fashions would have been nothing compared with the changes in social infrastructure. Over two decades, the rich had become richer, and the poor were much worse off than before. The threat of AIDS had put paid to the ethics of the 'free love' generation. Third World debt was mounting and, even in the so-called developed world, the free availability of credit was raging out of control. In the West, illegitimacy had changed from being a social stigma to become society's norm. And yet, any time traveller from the future would discern very little *real* (i.e. non-cosmetic) change in the West's churches over that period. The house church movement aside, little effort had been made to move with the times, and each local church was like a time capsule, holding out against the sea of change raging around its walls.

In whatever year of the late twentieth century Jean-Luc Picard chose to transport down to Earth, he would find a largely godless society, very different from the caring community aboard his starship. Though neither version of the *Enterprise* appears to have a chapel or chaplain, everyone seems to get along just fine without God. Hunger and poverty have been eliminated in the twenty-fourth century. Everyone has a job, a home, friendship. There is no sexism or racism; why, even those nasty Klingons are welcome at Star Fleet academy. Getting by without God has its price, though. Those characters we see on our television screens are bereft of free will, condemned to say the lines that the script-writers have written for the actors who play them!

Is such a Utopian society really possible? Perhaps. But to make it so will take more than a replicator machine to manufacture the kind of bonhomie that is required. The kind of medicine which can turn our real twentieth-century world into a kind and peaceful world is not found in the medical bag of a starship doctor. Many fraught communities bear closer resemblance to the dysfunctional crew of the *Red Dwarf* than that of either U.S.S. *Enterprise*.

There is no easy panacea for the world's ills. Christ is the answer, and the Church is the delivery system, but local Christians make up the labour force and all are finite people. A character in another cult TV sci-fi programme, *Third Rock From The Sun*, made a startlingly accurate summary of the human dilemma: 'These people have to make up life as they go along!' Transforming local communities is not done by any magic formula or science-fiction gizmo. It can be done only through the way everyday people live their daily lives, in the choices they make and in how the decisions they take modify their communities – for good or bad. Although we are constrained by the restrictions of our economic, cultural and social circumstances, we *do* have free wills. Life is not written out on some symphonic score; like free jazz, it's improvised.

Community Values

This all begs the questions of 'What is really meant by the word *community*?' It is a term laden with values that are not always shared by the various sociologists who seek to define the word. It often defies accurate definition, because people commonly take it to mean whatever they want it to mean! The only consensus is that it is a very 'good' and very 'positive' term; politicians drop it into their speeches because it makes people feel good, and economists use it as an antidote to privatisation and individualism. Put it in front of another word – as in, say, community care or community policing – and you have a term with a nice safe ring to it.

'Community' is sometimes used as a synonym for a local neighbourhood. Certainly before the Industrial Revolution the words would have been a good match. But the escalating mobility and ease of transport that has come increasingly to characterise modern life has led to mounting urbanisation. In large cities, people often bond with a sense of belonging that is non-geographical. People may feel a part of a 'community' that consists of a group of friends and acquaintances linked by common interests, say in the same sport or recreation, though they may all live miles apart. For others, their sense of 'community' might be tied to a caring network of old friends and relatives, though frequently they may now live hundreds of miles apart.

In South Asia, 'community' has always come from a sense of belonging to a particular sub-caste or group (of which there are some 5,000) depending on occupation, and bonded through family ties. This 'community' may comprise individuals and individual extended families that are spread across the length and breadth of the sub-continent; indeed, an Asian might feel part of a 'community' which stretches across the globe, even if there are no members of that 'community' (other than his or her own extended family) living within hundreds of miles.

In urban communities in the UK the concept of 'community' often has racist undertones, development worker Greg Smith believes:

> Where a neighbourhood has received migrants, established residents (the white working class) may feel their territory has been invaded and that the culture and bonds of their community have been eroded. The opportunity for neo-Nazis to mobilise around 'community' is greatest when the indigenous community is close knit, where deprivation is at its worst and when massive neighbourhood change is imposed from outside, for example in London Docklands in the early 1990's.

The whole notion of 'community' is often over-romanticised.

There is still a need for community workers to know the parameters of their community, perhaps by walking the streets and alleyways and learning the essential geographic boundaries, much in the same way that a detached youth worker would traditionally do, but also to be aware of the deeper defining characteristics of community. The worker must also tread the invisible conduits of cultures and belief systems. A 'community' tightly knit along lines of ethnicity, employment, economics, or political values may be geographically disparate. Ultimately, the community to which a person belongs (or would like to belong) is a matter which each individual must decide for him- or herself – though the range of options may be very constrained.

Church and Community

It's all very well to ask the academics the meaning of 'community', but what does the ordinary person in the street mean by the word? To most people it is an informal relational network, often linked to a specific location.

Some people regard their town or village as their community; but for the average Christian, the community to which they feel the greatest sense of belonging is their home church – or perhaps a group within that church. A person's sense of community might be family based, or it could be a network of local traders which a person regularly patronises. Three basic types of community are:

- **Functional** (a set of people to whom one relates for a specific task, e.g. business)
- **Geographical** (a set locality, with boundaries that are locational. i.e. bounded by streets, river, railway lines, etc.)
- **Relational** (a set of people with common bonds and ties, often family, but can also be some form of club)

If you are part of a community, you are no longer seen as an 'outsider'. Sometimes churches decide to hold a mission 'to the people of our area' – a concept which can be quite vague. The community is sometimes mistakenly seen as a *target* to which the church will *do* something, rather than a living network of people with whom they can *participate*. The unspoken purpose of the mission is to persuade people from other communities to join the church community; but full acceptance will be denied until the newcomer makes a profession of faith – or 'signs up for the theory'. For people who are not believers, the requirement to 'take on trust' the belief structure of the Church frequently presents an insurmountable hurdle.

In many cases, the sub-culture of our churches puts up false values which inhibit people from receiving the Gospel. Whereas Jesus was happy to go to the village watering hole and befriend a sexually-active unmarried woman, leading her in reflection about her life and offering her spiritual refreshment (the 'living waters'), the Church has been sometimes reluctant to have dealings with non-Christians until they are willing to blindly commit to a faith before they have the opportunity to see whether it works in practice. The cart has been put before the horse.

There is a mini-cab office next to Haddon Hall Baptist Church, south London. The drivers who wait there to ply their trade have no inclination to take part in any 'religious' activity, but their social consciences were pricked when the church asked them to drive a seven-ton truck to take relief to former Eastern-bloc countries, and they jumped at the opportunity. This was seen by them as a 'manly' activity of which they could be justly proud! Here the opportunity for reflection came as the truck was being driven across the continent, and Christians were able to lead the drivers in reflective thought. Churches would make better use of their resources if they were to put their evangelists alongside people in their local community, as they fulfil some socially useful task, rather than putting them in front of a congregation of Christians on a Sunday morning. If Mohammed will not go to the mountain, then the mountain will have to go to Mohammed, or to Rachel, or Lakshmi, or Jill, or Siddhartha.

'Meat and Potatoes'

The barriers that church sub-culture puts in front of people, that keep them from joining a church, are largely *community related*. Andrew Dilnot (Director of the Institute of Fiscal Studies, in London) explains that the plight of single parents, and the lone elderly, cannot be resolved by simply throwing money at the situation. But it *can* be addressed by drawing these isolated people into a community. For the reasons above, the Church is generally *ineffective* at drawing the lonely into its own community, because the cost of entry is viewed as too high a price. The lives of the poor can be better transformed once the Church has been transformed! Many Christians will know the frustration of trying to persuade their friends to accompany them to a Sunday service, and hearing a string of excuses week after week. Perhaps the underlying reason is that these people are being invited to come into a community to which they do not belong, and which will not accept them unless they make a Christian commitment.

One Christian organisation made its members feel exactly the same kind of alienation that an outsider would feel upon being brought into the unfamiliar environment of a church. On a tour of Bermondsey, they were made to go into a betting office, and to place a small bet on a race horse! 'But we can't do that! It's gambling!' 'Just regard it as the cost of this training exercise,' they were told. 'But I don't know what sort of people will be in there, I've never been in a betting shop before! I don't know what to *do*; how do I place a bet? What will happen to me?'

The second part of the exercise took place after the bets had been placed, as the Christians reflected on how they had felt in such an unfamiliar environment. The range of emotions – embarrassment, fear, uncertainty, anxiety – that they had experienced mirrored closely the emotions of someone going into a church for the first time: 'What sort of people will be in the church? Where will I sit? What do I do? When will I know if I'm supposed to be sitting, standing or kneeling? What about all the books that I get given at the door?' *The reflection was that this had been an intimidating experience, but an invaluable insight for Christians into what it feels like to be outside the church community.*

For non-Christians finding themselves in a new community, the entry point is often a visit to a local pub, where they wait desperately for an opportunity to develop a conversation with another individual or group. For a lone woman, this is not really an option. Christians can help in this situation, by showing vision and compassion. Churches can enable themselves to become part of the larger community through activities such as mums-and-toddlers clubs, lunch clubs, youth clubs, film evenings, women's suppers, men's breakfasts and the like. Not only are inroads made into the wider community, but members of that wider community are brought into the church building.

Such activities are generally viewed by a church as less important that the 'spiritual agenda' of Sunday services, Bible studies and prayer meetings, but in terms of fulfilling a mission to reach out to people who do not know God, these activities are among the most crucial and ought not to be neglected. They are the 'meat and potatoes' of Christian ministry, and just as digested food becomes a part of the body ('you *are* what you eat') these activities will help to transform the local church into a form that is truly the body of Christ. Then the congregation will begin to move from passively 'being' the church, to actively 'doing church' on the streets and byways. Faith will begin to move from the head to the heart; then from the heart to the hands and feet. The Church will start to become an agent of freedom and liberation, instead of . . .

The Church: An Instrument of Oppression?

'Hey! Did you know I'm the heavyweight boxing champion of the world?' says Super-dude.

'Yes, I know you've never seen me box; that's because I haven't! I'm so confident of my ability to outbox all comers that I've never bothered to strap on a set of boxing gloves, much less actually set foot in the ring!

'Perhaps you think I'm a bit presumptuous, my man; but I'm just like the Church really – too busy being pious to be bothered with the mundane matter of following Christ. . . .

'Have you noticed how many Christians – and particularly some Christian leaders – are so cocksure that everything they believe is doctrinally correct; that their interpretation of Scripture is the only valid option; and how they make the rest of us feel inadequate by their confidence of salvation? Can you dig it, some have probably already reserved their table for the wedding feast . . .

'Too busy being righteous to bother with the dirty ol' world, their books, talks and sermons often jive with highbrow intellectual ideas, man. But yo! Whenever I read the Gospels, this dude Jesus whom I meet is kind of at odds with the Church as we usually experience it. Hey! Perhaps Christ was unfortunate enough not to go to the right theological college . . .' quips Super-dude.

A browse through the Gospels reveals, not surprisingly, that believers can indeed be confident of their teaching on salvation – the atoning death of Christ and the grace of God may allow us to pray with confidence for the Holy Spirit to 'haunt us till we are innocent', to quote the poet Stewart Henderson. But a whole body of teaching seems often to get forgotten.

Try Matthew 25:34-36,40,41:

Come, you who are blessed by my father; take your inheritance, the kingdom prepared for you since the creation of the world. For I was hungry and you gave me something to eat, I was thirsty and you gave me something to drink, I was a stranger and you invited me in, I needed clothes and you clothed me, I was sick and you looked after me . . . I tell you the truth, whatever you did for one of the least of these brothers of mine, you did for me.

And, of course, those who do not do these things are told, 'Depart from me, you who are cursed, into the eternal fire prepared for the devil and his angels.'

God's passionate concern for the poor and needy is, sadly, often given little more than lip-service in some of the world's churches, by people who – in spite of their claims to take a high view of Scripture – seem to think that Christ was joking when he gave the above warning. God will judge, not according to what a person believes, but by the effect which the belief is allowed to have upon a person's outlook, choices, and actions.

It seems to many people that the Church has fallen into the trap of believing that its 'Sunday Worship' is really worship instead of a simple enactment of the real thing. Our hymns have become the burnt-offerings of Old Testament times, of which God pronounced himself to have had a bellyful. Our collections go to support the upkeep of buildings, rather than to God's real work of loving people into his Kingdom.

Churches in the West can learn a good deal from the churches in Latin America and Eastern Europe. Radical evangelicals in the former are bringing their faith directly to bear on the practical situations of oppression in which they find themselves, whilst East European churches are conspiring to bring benevolent social reform in the wake of communism.

'And what of the Church in the twenty-first century? Hey! Will it grasp the nettle of change, or continue on its path of self-delusion? Yo! Perhaps, for once, the leopard can change its spots . . .' grins Super-dude. 'I even promise to renounce my boxing title – if the Church will only promise to end its long years of oppressive behaviour. For God's sake.'

Working with Communities

Any positive approaches to issues such as unemployment, homeless-ness, violence, sexism, promiscuity, racism, crime, or drink and drug abuse can basically be summarised under the heading of Community Development, or community *renewal*, if you prefer. Development worker Greg Smith detects several different (though often overlapping) strands of community work practised by churches in the UK:

- There is a personal and pastoral response to local needs, which results in churches setting up projects such as soup kitchens, play centres, nurseries and lunch clubs, as a kind of 'First Aid' for the community.
- Others prefer to spend their time in political campaigning to attack the underlying roots of injustice.
- A third approach is for churches to apply for grants with which to hire professional workers to run full-time community projects.
- Some advocate practices developed in other parts of the world. In the Third World, 'enablers' (leaders who lead through service, doing as their congregations tell them) practise community development from the bottom up.

It is the latter approach which Greg finds the most exciting. There are grassroots theologians in the developing world who are exploring liberating 'new ways of being the Church', with an eager willingness to put theory into practice. In fact, with their immediate and direct responses to the specific social and historical situations faced by the individual churches, the theory often *follows* to describe the practice, rather than vice versa. Yet this is not as new or as radical as it may seem. In Britain in centuries past, the Franciscans, Lollards, Puritans, Quakers and Methodists had their own 'liberation theologies' long before the term was coined to describe the remarkable reformations that have occurred in South America since the sixties.

Stepping out in faith is often a risky business. When one small church opened an all-night coffee bar in a south-west London suburb, they hadn't bargained for the Mods and Hell's Angels fighting each other on the premises. 'We had someone faint in the club and when I asked a doctor to see her, he reported that she was suffering from malnutrition and chronic bronchitis. She was also pregnant, homeless and a drug addict,' one of the founders remembers. From this pastoral response to local need, the project quickly developed several full-time community projects, including an education unit, a hostel and a detoxification unit. *It has witnessed poverty in forms most Westerners don't even know exist.*

Sold Out?

But if the Church's role is simply that of a community developer, then has it not lost its evangelistic cutting edge? For such over-simplification to be true would mean a Church that met only people's physical needs. For a whole community's spiritual and emotional needs to be adequately addressed, the local church needs to be developing a vibrant *worshipping* community around itself. It is not necessary that everyone turns out for Sunday service, but essential that each individual within a healthy community is encouraged to meet with God at some point during the week. From that will grow a desire for culturally-relevant corporate worship.

Church growth models often see the Church's mission as the making of disciples, to enrich church life numerically and qualitatively. If society (mistakenly) thinks of Christians as simply 'people who seek to do good', then social action can be seen as useful. Fundamentalists may agree, for different reasons, seeking social action as a means to an end – meeting people to evangelise. Caring in the community is certainly good PR when it comes to gaining a high profile and increased credibility. Many churches have come to see social action as a legitimate part of their ministry, alongside evangelism and in equal partnership, as the two blades of a pair of scissors. More recently, though, many clergy and community workers have eschewed this potentially dualist model, in favour of a more harmonious 'holist' model, says Greg Smith: 'a seamless garment of mission'.

Such a seamless garment recognises that a person's spiritual needs cannot be separated from the emotional, social or physical aspects of life. Indeed, when expressed like this, it becomes obvious that emotional, social or physical suffering or deprivation will have a direct impact on the sense of spiritual well-being. What is required is the recognition that there are direct links and that people can be helped to make the connections. Such reflection presents entry points for change which have the potential for becoming truly redemptive.

There is a 'knock on' effect when a local church embraces issues of justice and reconciliation as part of a transforming agenda. *The church itself begins to be transformed in the process of working alongside the poor.*

This is a biblical model illustrated, for example, in Luke 18:35–43. Here Jesus encounters a blind man who calls out to him, and is rebuked by the crowd that is following Jesus. When he continues to call out, Jesus *asks the crowd to bring the man to him* and asks: 'What is it you want from me?' The blind man asks for his sight and Jesus heals him. The reaction of the crowd is fascinating. The people move from active *exclusion* of this upstart outsider, to praise, wonder, *inclusion* and changed expectation of their role.

They didn't previously appreciate that theirs was not a *passive* role, but rather that of *enablers* in Christ's ministry. Jesus used the crowd to help a person whom they actively did not want to associate with, and whom they actually told to be quiet. The crowd had to change their attitude before Jesus healed the blind man! If this is a picture of the Church today, *participation by those who had previously thought it was 'not their role' to get involved* will lead to changes in the situations of poor people. In other words, *the Church has to change itself as a pre-requisite to bringing good news.*

Let's make it so.

'Warp factor eight, Helmsman!

'Engage.'

Questions and Exercises

- How would *you* define the different communities represented in your own neighbourhood?
- How does your church relate to all the different locally represented communities?
- Are evangelism and social action like two blades of a pair of scissors, or more intimately connected?
- How should these considerations shape the ministry of the local church?
- Find out what your neighbours consider to be the most pressing needs of your own community.

2

Participation

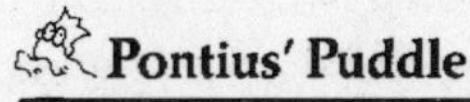

It's going to be the biggest birthday 'bash' that the world has ever known, but it seems as though the person whose birthday it commemorates is not welcome at his own party! It's taking place at venues all across the globe, many of which have been booked years ahead. There will be exhibitions, jamborees, perhaps even a giant Ferris wheel. The cost will be astronomical. If you're poor, then tough luck, because *you* won't be there. But you'll be in good company; Jesus Christ hasn't been invited either – and it's *his* birthday!

As the year 2000 approaches, the globe is gripped by PMT – Pre-Millennial Tension. Some pundits predict that the new millennium will mark the commencement of some kind of Golden Age for humanity, but the idea is certainly no more than wishful thinking as far as the destitute are concerned. For them, every year passes by very much like the last – but this is not God's will. His holy laws – given to Moses on Mount Sinai – call for a special *Year of Jubilee* to be celebrated every fifty years, as a time of relief for those in the thralls of poverty. It's a feast to look forward to!

25

God commanded that land should not be sold in perpetuity, but only the use of that land leased for a set number of years. When the Year of Jubilee rolled around, all debts were to be cancelled, and the land returned to the 'freeholder' family whose heritage it represented. (It's all there in Leviticus 25:8–55.) However poor a person was, he or she would know that their condition was only temporary; in the modern world, there is no such reprieve, and the poor are locked into their poverty for a life sentence.

The key that might release them is something called a community development initiative.

What *is* Community Development?

'Community development is a way of working which seeks to do two things,' explains Marilyn Taylor of the secular approach, in her useful little booklet *Signposts to Community Development*.

> First, it seeks to release the potential within communities (what the business world might call 'added value'). It does this by bringing people together to address issues of common concern and to develop the skills, confidence and resources to address these problems.
>
> Secondly, it works where necessary to change the relationships between people in communities and the institutions that shape their lives. Its aim in doing so is to ensure that communities and the people within them are recognised as partners in production, services and democratic life rather than the objects of decisions and policies made elsewhere.'

In one sentence: It is a method or approach concerned with the *change* and *growth* of communities. (These methods will include: consultations, outreach, profiling, policy analysis, devolution, co-ordination, networking, organising, resourcing, negotiating, and other long words. The goal is *transformation*.)

The phrase 'community development' itself is falling into misuse as practitioners begin to see the implication that they themselves are 'developed' whilst the community to which they are seeking to relate is somehow 'backward' and in need of their expertise. This expression 'transformation' is becoming a more popular alternative, because of its absence of negative connotations. In a Christian context, this transformation will always include a spiritual element, challenging the values to which people adhere once they have the freedom to make choices.

When commuters organise a car pool, or young mothers put together a baby-sitting rota, they may not know it but they are 'doing community development'! Their aims will be a medley of the following: providing mutual support; engaging in shared activity; fighting outside threats; gaining influence; providing local services; reinforcing a common identity; and giving individuals a keen sense of belonging.

The process of planned social change does not take place overnight. It usually requires a skilled motivator to work over long periods with infinite patience, often with the backing of external support agencies. Change is *organic*, gradually substituting 'self-reliant activeness' for the passive expectation of assistance from a third party. For example, instead of *giving* someone a fish, you teach them *how* to fish – and then empower them to get their own fishing rights! You don't just give medical relief, you train doctors and nurses to give a sustainable medical service. *Community transformation is not concerned with welfare hand-outs, its aim is to make the developer redundant by enabling the community and the individuals within it successfully to control their own destiny.*

It's like a child growing up, moving from babyhood – with total reliance upon a mother figure for even its most basic requirements – to gradually taking on responsibility for washing, dressing and feeding itself, then becoming a partner in its own education, eventually achieving complete financial independence. Good development programmes do not come 'off the shelf'. They are 'custom built' to take account of the local setting. Local benefactors are encouraged to 'look sideways' to see what they can do together, in full *partnership* with their peers.

For example, Donna, a black psychiatric nurse, became concerned about the large numbers of black people, mainly men, with mental problems in her area of Birmingham. Her own desire to do something to help has inspired her church. They are now extending their building to include rooms for counselling to try to address some of the problems, and to intervene before people reach a crisis point.

Then there's Deirdre. She became a Christian in prison, through the ministry of the prison chaplain, who was also the minister of her local church. Now, some years later, Deirdre works as a Community Development Worker, building bridges between that church and the local school and community. She and the church are participating in the process of setting up a project to provide support for ex-offenders as they re-adjust to life outside.

Bottoms Up!

For community development to produce effective transformation within a particular place, it is often necessary for the power structures to be examined, and for changes to take place within them.

It is essential for social infrastructures and community facilities to be developed *locally*, encouraging local decision making, and making the local community a 'stakeholder' with interest in the development work. This is termed a 'bottom-up ' approach, and it is preferable to structures being imposed upon a community from outside, by those with power over the community, in a draconian 'top-down' manner.

There are still potential dangers of the bottom-up model. Just as increased home-ownership has meant security for some and repossession for others, so choices in education enable some parents to send their children to the best schools while other parents lamentably find themselves left with whatever remains once the best places have been taken. Powerlessness is often reflected in the ease with which those in the middle or near to the bottom act as a net to intercept benefit intended for those who are really at the bottom! *Casting an individual in the role of a consumer of community resources may leave the poor and powerless at the mercy of market forces that they do not understand and cannot control.*

It may help to understand the process if we look at what happens when the process described above is *not* followed. Typically, a local council may attempt to address the problems of a run-down estate by putting in a few flower beds to make the neighbourhood look more attractive. Though introducing beauty into an area can often be useful to the transformation process, it is not an end in itself. It looks nicer, but it has achieved little impact on all the underlying problems which still exist below the surface. If the people of the area are not adequately consulted, they will not 'own' the initiative, which they may quickly come to believe has been foisted upon them. The flower beds may soon become vandalised. 'We tried to do our best, but look what the locals did. There's no pleasing some people,' the authorities will say, and probably proceed to ignore the problem area.

Efforts that are not *participatory*, and which are not undertaken in full *consultation* with those whom the measures are intended to assist, are almost certainly doomed to failure. It's not good enough to do things *for* people, as occurred in the 1970s and 80s, much less to do things *to* people as occurred in the 1950s and 60s; we must do things *with* the people. The world has moved on in its social thinking, while the Church has not. *The Christian needs to engage with the world as it now is – not as it once was!*

Change of Thinking

Local churches often need to begin to think *developmentally* and to animate their local communities out of a sense of genuine concern – not simply because Christians view their neighbours as potential pew fodder. If a church seeks to run a welfare project solely as a means of making contacts with people whose souls it wants to save, then it is probably doomed to failure. The approach is a million miles from the *participatory* concepts which, rightly, are currently in vogue. If someone goes into their local church, will they have an opportunity to speak to someone about God? *No!* Typically they will have the opportunity to sit there while someone stands at the front and explains what they *ought* to think about God! Christians are often fond of making statements, rather than asking questions.

Yet, when we read in the Bible about the conversation following the Fall near the beginning of Genesis, we do not find that God makes statements to Adam and Eve, he simply asks questions of them. His approach is participatory, until after he hears the hapless pair blame the serpent, each other, and *God himself* for their situation: 'It's all the fault of that woman that *you* gave me, God!' Adam retorts. 'You're the one to blame, God, not me!' Only after Adam and Eve have refused to take *responsibility* for their situation, and for the actions that have brought it about, is God judgmental towards them! (If only they had said 'It was our fault, God,' then they might have avoided the alienation and separation that resulted.)

For a church to open a coffee bar or a drop-in centre for its local community is a great step forward, but for many, the *motivation* may be suspect. If the aim is simply to draw passers-by into a church building, to sow the seeds for evangelism in the hope that a purely *spiritual* transformation can be brought about at a later stage, then the venture may be doomed from the onset. Local churches by the hundred have tried this, but usually – though the doors are open day after day, week after week – the anticipated evangelism never happens, because the moment Christians begin to 'preach' to their customers, the customers all go off somewhere else to get a cup of tea, for a quiet life. But if a church opens its doors intent to meet the spiritual, *emotional*, *mental*, and *physical* needs of hurting people in their locality – and is prepared to adopt a servant attitude towards its clientele, allowing its hurting customers to take the lead and to bring their own agendas – then here is a worthy aspiration that is far more likely to bear rich fruit in the long term.

'We see our mission as being the creation of goodwill within the community,' says John Matthews, pastor of Ruchill Parish Church in urban Glasgow:

Out of that goodwill comes the opportunity to allow people to explore their faith further. They may not see themselves as doing that, but there is a great interest in spirituality today, for a whole range of reasons: because of people being hurt; people living in broken families and communities; people who are well-to-do with jobs and good health, but finding a loss of meaning and purpose in their lives.

For all of those reasons, people explore spirituality and, in the process of doing that, they think of the Church. They may *attempt* the Church, or they may previously have attempted the Church, but either way they find that it is irrelevant. It doesn't *inform* their faith. It doesn't help them to explore their spirituality. They will then look for other things, perhaps within the New Age Movement. They will pick up a spirituality that is an amalgam of horoscopes, second-hand reports of near-death experiences, information gleaned from Dennis Potter plays and other things from television, in a whole mish-mash of counterfeit spirituality. The Church isn't helping them to explore, and therefore their spirituality is not rooted or founded in biblical spirituality, as we understand it.

At his own church, John sees a way forward:

We are looking to engage with people in a way that is friendly and that helps them to feel comfortable. We try to bring them to an understanding of God through Jesus Christ, which is much more difficult. People are reluctant to come to a church for the principal act of public worship; it is alien to them. At a typical 11.00 a.m. service, the doors have to be locked because of potential vandalism – and because of the chilly draughts! There the people are – they're captives! Often it's an hour of the minister doing everything, with very little congregational participation.

How do you take the message of the Gospel six foot beyond the walls of the church? 'Being church', for us, is coming together to worship. Too many conservative evangelicals are obsessed with the notion of being fed and nurtured, and of cultivating their personal Christian faith – to the extent that people move to different churches if they don't get nurtured. We're seeing more and more 'gathered' congregations, where people pass the door of three or four parish churches, to land at the door of some conservative evangelical gathering, whose pastor is a wonderful Bible teacher.

It's all me, me, me. ME, ME, ME! Dahling, the Bible Study groups here are absolutely *fabulous*. That new curate is simply *divine* . . .

The Bad Samaritan

In this situation, Christians are not relating to people in the area where they are living. Their neighbours are strangers. They may speed through the town or city on their way to work, or to socialise with friends, when a hundred yards to each side of the road lies an entirely different environment with which they are totally unfamiliar. There is no *participation* in the lives of these needy people by the transiting Christians. John Matthews says:

They are quite oblivious to the *horror* in which people are living, just a short distance away from the main thoroughfare. If you were to tell them about it, they would be astonished. They might want to offer money, or prayer, but if you asked them to help in any practical way, they would have to say, 'But I wouldn't know what to do!' or 'I couldn't handle that.' When you tell them the stories of some of the young children or families, of how they come to be in these dreadful circumstances, they find it un-believable. Yet there is a great proportion of the population living in these difficulties. *And we say that the Gospel is good news to the poor* . . .

I'd like to know, from the poor people, how *they* see the Gospel as being good news for them. And, if it *is* good news, why aren't they flocking to hear it? Is it our inability to present it properly? Is it their perception of what we are presenting? The Bible says that the common people heard Jesus gladly. What was it about him that was different from the kind of preaching and teaching in which we are involved today? We need to find the answers to these questions.

The Church is good at looking after its own members, so long as they conform to expectations. The common people seem to have given up on the Church, but they have not given up on God. Their understanding of God is often warped, twisted and false, but they don't come to church to get those perceptions straightened. If they won't come to a church, then church must go to them. John believes that the only way forward is for Christians to become a true part of their communities. This may involve street work or a visiting programme, with real encounters and actual engagement with people.

Unfortunately, many churches perform this task via a leaflet distribution, or by taking around a church magazine. In doing this, they succeed only in telling people where the church is located, times of services, and the range of activities on its programme. We tell people where the church is at: 'This is when *we* are available. This is where you can contact *us*. Here's a list of *our* organisations. If you want God and Jesus, an exploration of your faith, here it is!' Rather than, 'Where are *you* at?'

The 'Death' of God

Most literature outreach by local churches is the equivalent of sending out a ransom note, made up from letters and words cut out of a newspaper: '*Okay, we've got God. If you want him, here is our list of demands.*' Instead of: 'Leave your life savings in a brown paper envelope behind the cistern at Victoria Station,' the message is: 'Leave your life in our hands. Come to our service and put some money in the collection. After fifteen years you might have earned your way into some minor position of responsibility. Keep taking the bread and wine, stay quiet and don't tell anybody, or God gets bumped off!'

The Church needs to look through the eyes of the people that it is trying to reach, not through the perception of those that have *already* been reached.

The problem is not solely one that affects poor areas. The up-market areas of town have their problems too, though often of a very different nature. To use a golfing analogy, you must play the ball 'where it lies'. For many people, the ball lies in the deep rough. We might want it to be on the fairway, or on the putting green, but it's actually in a nettle bed or behind a clump of bushes! Our theological tools are not equipped for the deep rough, John Matthews believes:

> We are used to using putters, to make converts of people who are already close to some idealised notion of what a nice respectable Christian should be like. Putters are effective with those who already 'have their life in order' when they come looking for God in a church. For those whose lives are out of control, you need a much steeper iron, and the ball may still not oblige you by chipping on to the green – it may slice off into deeper rough. Some of the more conservative evangelicals naively expect people to come to Christ and to have a straight behavioural path, getting more Christ-like each month as sanctification takes place.

We're fond of hearing testimonies in which people come to God and are set free immediately from the chains of drink, drugs, promiscuity and other habits. In practice, the tangled mess they have made of their lives in terms of personal relations and dependencies stays with them. Sorting out these problems takes time, but in the interim the well-spoken person from a good home has the skills to 'cover up' the true situation. 'But in my territory,' says John, 'what you see is what you get. There is no affectation or embellishment.' None the less, there will be *judgment* upon them from people from the suburbs, who can hide their own faults and failings behind their lace curtains.

They won't get their act together unless they come into contact with the Church. 'That's where they belong,' says the evangelical, 'in our building, where our minister preaches a wonderful Gospel message!' But if people are *not* coming into the building, how are we to deal with the impasse? John Matthews tackled the problem by setting up a Tea Room, as a daytime witness, a chance for people to enter a friendly atmosphere for a cup of home-made soup, a filled roll or a mug of tea: 'In that atmosphere, there is a better chance to get to know people, and, in the getting to know them, perhaps make them less anxious about coming to meetings that are in the church and *of* the church.'

Stepping Stones

People stop John at funerals; they shake hands and say: 'Minister, I've been to your church.' He looks at them, knowing he's never seen them before. They say, 'Sure, I've been to your Tea Room.' To them, the Tea Room *is* church. John ponders how to make the Tea Room more of a church, or how he can have *stepping stones* that lead from the informal Tea Room atmosphere to the beginnings of a journey of faith. We can 'kid ourselves along' with social action, to the point that it is all we ever do. But the essence of the Gospel is changed behaviour, and changed values – a process sustained by the Spirit of God in hearts and minds. 'People have to come into contact, not only with Christian volunteers in the Tea Room and sense their warmth and welcome, but with the claims of the Gospel – whether in a church or the Tea Room is not important.'

There is a cost involved, in putting right relationships, and in discontinuing activities that are hurtful and harmful to themselves and others. It is a behavioural matter, and in the Bible we see Jesus creating the goodwill into which he can bring God's standards. When he met the woman at the well, it was *she* who brought up religion, not him. All Christ did was to ask her for a drink of water, for goodness' sake! Jesus spent time with her in an environment with which she was familiar, and where she felt comfortable; he achieved great changes in her life, but the disciples – like some conservative churchmen today – were *horrified* by such an unconventional approach. Eating and drinking with sinners? Jesus's response was to say, 'The Son of Man came eating and drinking and you say, "Here is a glutton and a drunkard, a friend of tax collectors and 'sinners'." But wisdom is proved right by all her children' (Luke 7:34, 35). The proof of the pudding is in the eating!

A sixteen-year-old girl had taken a massive overdose on the streets of Glasgow. When John pointed out that she should be careful since she had her whole life ahead of her, she retorted, 'Why should I? My life is full of shit! I'm off to get some more tablets to finish it off.' Here was a real *entry point* into this vulnerable young woman's mixed-up life. It would have been futile to take her on a Bible study or to preach morality to her. The only option was to address her physical and emotional predicament – to let her set her own agenda, and to participate in her life as much as she would allow. Yet, where does evangelism stop and social concern begin? If evangelism is the 'proclamation of the good news' then the good news for this young woman is that she is dearly loved by the loving God who wants her for his child, regardless of the state her life might be in. Then there is no distinction as to whether care and concern for the person comes under the heading of social concern or evangelism; the two are both ingredients in the same tasty pudding!

Let people tell their stories of their own community and their part within it. Given half a chance, many poor and lonely people will talk for hours: 'I remember when . . .' To jump in with a well-meant Bible quotation and the response: 'Never mind all these stories; what you need is Jesus,' is facile and ineffectual. Only a seamless concern for a person's physical, mental, spiritual and emotional well-being is adequate to bridge the gulf that exists in most people's lives. Let them grieve for their lost opportunities, and for the way their lives might have panned out *'if only'*. People are seldom more themselves than when they are talking of their lifetime's experience. When somebody begins to feel that their experiences have actually been worthwhile, have made them the person they are today, and are of interest to someone else, then the process of transformation can begin to take place.

You develop a community by developing the people within it, and that is a costly process. There is no place for Christians who at best see themselves as fairy godmothers, misusing God like a magic wand, so that the poor can immediately become Cinderella at the ball. In real life, it takes patience, participation and hard work to bring about transformations – magic wands are in short supply!

Change of Heart

If you go to South London and talk to the people of Bermondsey – in those parts that the bombs missed during the last war – they will tell you of the thriving community life which once existed, and the sense of community which is not shared by the present generation. There is not much cohesion left now; the elderly reminisce while the unemployed young people score their drugs, the middle-aged contemplate their prospects of a second or third marriage, and the children learn how to survive on the streets. But there are signs of hope. Single parents work with young people in one secular project, helping others to avoid the mistakes that they themselves have made. Yet these unmarried mothers seldom set foot in a church building more than once, such is the level of condemnation that they feel from the Christians there. Physical and emotional needs are being addressed, but the Church's intimidating attitude has prevented the spiritual needs from being reached. They see Christians as people who have 'got their own lives sorted out', and who appear to 'look down' upon those who haven't.

'We have a score or more of men who drink under the bridge of the nearby canal,' says John Matthews, in Glasgow. 'Some have homes, while others are *skippering* or sleeping rough. They have a fortnight's growth on their chin, and dribble down the front of their sweaters.' John tells the story of meeting one vagrant who said, 'Once I've got my life together, I'm going to come to your church.' John replied, 'No you won't. And what's more no one in the church has got their life together either. Come now, just as you are, because the Church is for sinners like you *and* me. Why don't you cut the nonsense and start joining in.' Later, addressing a group of Christians, John asked, 'Who is responsible for projecting this image that people have to get their lives sorted out before they can join a church?'

As we have said, change comes about through *participation*. It is wrong to see this process as functioning in one direction only: that outsiders will be changed if they participate in the local church. *If a church participates in the local community, the church will be changed too.* Many churches are frightened of change: 'Oh no, we might become more liberal. The social gospel will rear its ugly head again.' In fact, through community participation, opportunities for reflection and evangelism increase dramatically. Participation will *force* a church to evaluate its evangelistic strategy to cope with the increased influx of local people. As members of the local community come to reflect upon – and to re-evaluate – their own values through contact with church members, bridges will be built across which people will be able to cross into the Kingdom of God. Then Jubilee can truly come to them at last.

A long-term unemployed man in Newcastle gained self-confidence and a renewed vigour for living, as a result of being asked to help as a volunteer in a charity shop run by a local church. Since he has begun to do this work, he has met far more people than would otherwise have been the case; he feels happier in himself; and he has now become a Christian. The church said, 'We value what you can do, so please come and do it with us.' *The opportunity to participate* was the overriding factor in his decision to enter God's Kingdom.

Soup runs, entertainment programmes in old people's homes, interior decoration for the destitute, are other opportunities to introduce non-Christians into the church community. Let them say, 'Well, I'm not interested in the religious bit, but I want to help out in this wonderful work that you are doing.' This meeting of people's personal needs seems to have been the facet that most attracted people to Christ's own ministry. The teaching and the miracles were important too, but it was his *concern for people* that was the major transforming force that he wielded in the lives of individuals.

Sunday services are seldom the most appropriate meetings to

which to invite non-Christian friends. Those services should primarily serve to encourage believers; not to provide an audience of Christians to watch in morbid fascination as an evangelist attempts, not too subtly, to convert the one or two non-Christians he has spotted, and who are eyeing the door to make a quick getaway. As many churches have one Sunday service that is well attended and a second which garners only a luke-warm turnout, it might be an idea for churches to make their second service into a 'user friendly' meeting for enquirers. Some Christians who have tried it say: 'Perhaps you should have a bar at the back, or let people bring their beer in!' You could even 'go the whole hog' and have the service in an upstairs room of your local pub, where visitors might feel more comfortable.

Church buildings are often daunting architectural edifices which are totally alien to today's young people; though older people are inclined to be grateful that the church is the only building in the area that has escaped the developers' bulldozer. For them, the old building represents a stable link with a nostalgic past that has now been taken from them. A balance needs to be struck.

This process of reconnecting local churches with ordinary people is not simply a rehearsal of old dogma. It is the process of staying a step ahead of a changing world.

Not Me, Guv!

Trends in modern psychology have led people to believe that they are not to blame for their own situation. It is all the fault of their mother for taking them from the breast too early; their father for not being there enough; their teacher for his sexist attitude; their boyfriend for not wearing a condom; or the council for not providing a ground floor flat on a nice estate.

No one is willing to take *responsibility* for their own lives any longer. 'If only my potty training had been better! If only I'd gone to the right school! If only I'd met the right girl . . .' The welfare state has bred a dependency culture that allows people to continue in that sort of negative and unconstructive thinking. 'It's social security's fault that I haven't got any money.' The alienation is effectively summed up by the Pink Floyd on their classic rock album *The Wall*. Here, lyricist Roger Waters is saying, 'I'm a miserable old so-and-so and it's all the fault of everyone but me. It's *their* fault that I've had to build this wall of isolation around myself.'

The way forward is to *consult* with these people, and to give them a voice in how they want their lives to change, *and* in the process by which this is to be achieved. This rings alarm bells for some Christians: 'We can't let outsiders have a say in what takes place in our church, or they'll be replacing Sunday worship with Bingo sessions!' Here the Church is joining in the 'turning away' from the poor and downtrodden, for fear of the consequences of becoming 'involved'. Often, the worst possible scenario is imagined, and used as an excuse to prevent anyone else from bringing their own agenda into the building that the local church owns and is determined to hang on to for grim death!

No one is willing to face up to the question, 'What does it mean to *be* a church?' The issue of consultation is a parallel one which provides the programme and the platform on which the evangelistic – the transforming vehicle – can occur. A local church – if it is to *be* a truly local church – needs to ask the community, and to explore with local people, their own perception of the underlying problems within the neighbourhood. The fact that the church may be unable to bring in its own evangelistic agenda every ten minutes should *not* always be viewed as a problem!

Here are three approaches to how churches can relate to their local community. There is the frequently-used *prescriptive* model of church where the church identifies the people's problem and does something about it, to the people. Most churches never get beyond (if they even reach) the *consultative* model: 'We'll go out and refer to the community to work out the best way of pursuing an agenda which is owned by the church members rather than the local community.' Then there is the *participatory* model, which allows ordinary local people to own the process of identifying the needs of an area, designing the solutions and evaluating the impact.

The reason why this latter way of 'going about things' is so positive is that it deploys Christians, not simply as people who appear to be peddling a theory of personal spirituality, but as compassionate people with clues as to how real solutions can be found to real issues. They become people who give the powerless person a hearing, thereby earning respect. The Gospel is seen to make practical sense. Jesus is seen as someone who can be admired by even the most cynical person.

Ann Morisy, Community Ministry Adviser for CARIS in the Diocese of London, in *Beyond the Good Samaritan* distinguishes 'community ministry' from 'individual pastoral care'. 'For the most part, pastoral care is reactive, since it involves responding to a problem associated with an individual (often in confidence). Community ministry, by contrast, is proactive in that it involves . . . an assessment of the pressures acting upon a local community and envisages . . . a corporate response.'

Morisy continues: 'The commitment to dialogue must be a priority within community ministry.' Even those who are housebound can take on a 'prayer burden', i.e. 'to listen and reflect on the pain of others that almost at times fills the news.'

Discussion groups can uncover the issues and get the community to think about them – but the solution that the community proposes may initially be anathema to the church members. One church-run AIDS programme worked brilliantly through its discussion and reflection stages, but when the community was asked, 'What do you want to *do* about the AIDS problem in your area?' it responded, 'We want more condoms.' The church needed to work through the implications of providing condoms with the inevitable increase in casual sexual relations that was likely to follow.

Some of the Christians considered that the risk to human life from the AIDS virus legitimised the provision of condoms, though there was dissent from others. At the very least, the dilemma provided an entry point for further discussion within the church and community alike. The question to be asked was, 'What is it about the way people are relating to each other in this neighbourhood that promiscuity should be so rampant?' Further discussion revealed that the local men were prone to getting drunk in a particular bar and then going off to find themselves a liaison for the night, and that this was the accepted practice. The church asked, 'What do the local women feel about this situation? Is this demand for condoms the result of the loudest people in the local community – the men – being the only ones to be heard? Or is it the women who want the condoms, to be protected from their promiscuous husbands? Where do the innocent children stand in all of this?'

The choice of approach, and the understanding that a church can come to about the approach it wishes to take, are crucial steps. Identifying the right approach is vital if the correct developmental pathway is to be found. It's a long, slow process to get Cinderella ready for the party.

Into the Danger Zone

Ownership is a critical issue. It is possible for a church to go too far down the participatory route, and to lose sight of the transforming influence that Christians need to bring to bear. Many projects have commenced with a very clear Christian agenda, and which a local community has 'bought into', only for the church to hand the project over to the community. Once the majority of voices on the Management Committee are non-Christian and the project has become secularised, then an opportunity has been lost for positive Christian witness. There are often good grounds for a church to try to keep hold of the transforming agenda.

Amazingly, Everton Football Club started as a church youth football team, but clearly any church agenda has long since disappeared! Shelter was set up as a national housing charity by a group of British Christians, but it quickly lost its overt biblical agenda in exchange for a 'right on' left-wing agenda. The Christian agenda needs to be 'How can we actually transform lives?' rather than 'How can we hang on to ownership of this project?' If you transform lives, then hand the project over to those people whose lives have been transformed, then nothing is lost.

Generally, outsiders do not want to join (or participate in) a body over which they have no control; much less one which they believe is constipated with ancient hierarchies, or incontinent with historical patterns of worship which spill out like gibberish! Our churches are easily trapped into programmes which are suppressive and culturally determined. They alienate the unchurched through forms of expression which are outdated. Old Victorian hymns have no relevance to most people who have grown up listening to rock or dance music. Even tunes from *Mission Praise* and the like can sound corny and twee to young people who listen to hip-hop, acid house and rap – and who go to acid house parties. The Kingdom of God needs a church *of* the poor – a mutually supportive group of believers who are committed to impacting on the wider society around them – not a church *for* the poor. Non-believers need to be facilitated to reach a place where they feel they belong, *before* they are expected to make a committment to Jesus Christ.

But where *is* such a church? How does one start? Perhaps we need to begin with a *core group*: the existing churches. Christians need metaphorically to 'take the walls off' their churches, to achieve openness and transparency. They need to start sharing stories and experiences, and bring biblical reflection, values and understanding to situations, rather than studying Scripture in isolation from everyday life.

Already, a new way of 'doing theology' is developing, from innovators who are travelling light without the accumulated baggage of previous generations. The institutional Church is frequently seen as being on the side of the oppressors: the old joke about it being the Tory party at prayer comes easily to mind! Culturally relevant worship, a prophetic voice with which to contextualise the Gospel, and a new commitment to networking are beginning to flourish. House churches, black Pentecostal churches, community-based congregations (such as Canning Town's Mayflower Family Centre) are good examples of God 'doing a new thing'.

Churches sometimes think that every project they set up will last for ever. In practice, most development projects last for five or ten years, and then different needs will usually come to the surface.

The Holy Spirit is the spirit of life, who is constantly doing new things. Christians are simply called to be 'faithful in the present moment', and to leave the future in God's capable hand. Then the party can really get under way.

Bottoms up!

Questions and Exercises

- How do you think your local community views your church?
- How prepared is your church to address the pastoral risks and issues which arise through a greater level of *participation* in ministry throughout the church?
- What are the benefits and drawbacks of 'travelling light', as suggested two paragraphs from the end of the chapter?
- What are the similarities, and differences, between your church and John Matthews' church?
- Write a letter to your MP or other representative, expressing concern for a local issue.

3

Reflection

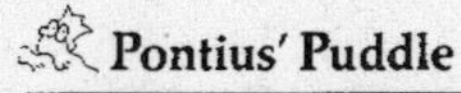

From space, the Earth's blue oceans seem to play hide-and-seek with the planet's swirling white clouds of water vapour. Here, in contrast to the hydrogen seas of the outer gas planets, or the deadly carbon dioxide of the other inner planets, organic life is possible. Of the millions of species to whom the earth is 'home', only one sentient species can feel shame – or needs to . . .

Ever since the Fall, our societies have been characterised by inequality and injustice. People often continue to treat each other in a manner that is scarcely better than that of beasts. From Buenos Aires to Bombay, London to Los Angeles, it seems that the rich continue to get richer, while the poor don't simply get poorer – in many cases they actually roll over and die from malnutrition, disease and neglect.

The chief distinction is no longer between the First and the Third World, it is between the 'haves' and the 'have nots' which exist in every country on the globe. Though we are all one family sharing one world, we don't often behave like it. At best, we're like selfish siblings who squabble at the meal table over who will have the biggest portion, or a bickering couple who have long since fallen out of love and who are acrimoniously carving up their shared belongings.

'Poverty may wear a different face in different countries, but its effects are much the same: isolation, depression, powerlessness, rejection, and lack of opportunity,' according to the *Neighbours UK Action Pack* produced by Tear Fund.

Jesus interacted discerningly with the people around him – those whom he searched out, as well as those who crossed his path. His answers were never glib, nor predictably the same for everyone. He treated people as individuals, and their needs where they were. Like Jesus, UK Action – and other Christian bodies like it – believes in bringing good news to the poor, some of whom are standing in our hallways or sleeping in our doorways.

Jesus was never accused of patronising anyone. He was never accused of being moralistic, either. In our thoughtful response to people who are stigmatised by poverty, we should not 'keep our distance' – we must not increase their burden by making them feel patronised. Rather, we ought to be identified with them, as one of them, living alongside them, bringing the hope of lasting change. We are not 'worlds apart'. We are all passengers on Spaceship Earth, though some travel *first* class and others *third* class. With a bit of effort, we can all travel *second* class.

For Richer, for Poorer

In July 1996, the *UN Development Report* revealed the startling fact that the gap between rich and poor in the British Isles exceeded that in Nigeria, Jamaica and Ethiopia. It was ironic that a country with such a rich history of 'commonwealth' should have within it such an appalling level of inequality, with so little of its great wealth actually held 'in common'! Though it's an inescapable fact that for many people in Britain the standard of living has improved over the 1980s and 90s, for a significant group of people, there has been the dehumanising experience of being trapped below the poverty threshold – an experience of hopeless dependency of which the majority simply have no first-hand experience.

Even those with wealth can feel 'trapped'. Theirs is not a dependency on handouts from others, but on the relentless need to keep earning money at a furious pace. Though the standard of living continues to rise, the cost to people, families and communities also rises. As Christian author Tom Sine notes, the cost of the dream of wealth and security is getting higher for each generation. *Have we mortgaged the future to pay for the present?* If so, let's reflect on the kind of world that will be left for our children – and our children's children – to live upon . . .

The 'leaner' Britain which the Thatcher and Major eras encouraged has left many people feeling that something is going seriously wrong with society. Many would love to be able to help with the homeless; the elderly; and those for whom the experience of dysfunctional families is little more than a living hell. But after their own kids are clothed and fed; after the hours are put in at work; after this and that commitment has been met, there simply isn't space left in the timetable for such matters. Many well-intentioned people – Christians and non-believers alike – feel the sense of frustration.

Eddie Grundy, in that time-honoured radio soap *The Archers*, served up, at the end of 1996, a homily enough to make any upper lip quiver. When his evil landlord Pemberton announced that this tenant farming family was to be turned off the land, Eddie told his fretting wife that Pemberton would never win, because they had friends who valued them in the village – friends who would never stand idle and see them become destitute. They had each other, and while that solidarity remained, they would not lose their fight to remain in the village. Trite and sentimental it was, but a salient reminder that relationships form the mainstay of communities still today.

The lesson is that, corny as it sounds, *people need people*. There is solidarity in numbers. Those who have the resources but no time can work alongside those who have time but no resources. A partnership is possible, through which rich and poor alike can strive together for a better world, ruled by godly values. Martin Luther King's dream is still some way from becoming a reality, but with hope in our hearts and friends at our side, we may yet see a more just and equal society. The old song 'reach out and touch somebody's hand' was never more relevant.

The Battle Cry

Now is the time for candid reflection on the state of society, and for action – before society becomes so materialistic and individualistic that our doors are always firmly bolted, to keep the little we have from the clutches of those who have even less, and we are left with only our paranoia for company.

The Church has stood indomitably in the past for values diametrically opposed to these trends. As an institution, it has spoken of community and reconciliation. It has stood for the eternal values of forgiveness, love, peace, justice and equality of opportunity. It has prized the value of humanity, regardless of what a person 'does' in terms of occupation. At the level of the local church, however, there is currently – in most cases – little being lived out that is *distinctive in terms of visible signs of different values.*

Instead, there is a potent cocktail of the following three ingredients: the heresy that 'wealth is automatically a sign of God's blessing'; the notion that Christianity is chiefly about how 'I' can get through 'my' life in one piece; and the lie that Christianity is more of an abstract philosophy than a radical way of life. It has led to that dreadful state of affairs where the Church is neither hot nor cold, and is danger of being spat out by God! (See Revelation 3.) A vivid picture indeed, for a society which picks up the latest fashion one day and discards it the next.

The Church has much to offer to a fallen world, but it has much to *receive* too, from those outside its ancient walls, who want to know God but who are not initially interested in doctrine. They yearn for a rich spiritual life, but not on the self-serving terms offered by the institutional Church. They long to belong, but feel unaccepted by religious people who seem to put more emphasis on solemn ritual, or upon clappy-happy 'worship', than upon deep relationships with real people in their own neighbourhood.

People today often have 'attitude', but churches don't understand this euphemism for the self-confident projection of a forceful personality; it's not 'submissive' enough for Christians to approve of it. People today live in a culture whose tastes, views and opinions are shaped mainly through fashion, music, television, films, and other media, including – increasingly – the Internet; churches only appear to understand the staid church sub-culture that is confined within the four walls of the church building. ('What's an internet?')

Scripture Grenades

In his highly-recommended book *I Believe in Taking Action*, Steve Chalke says, 'The Church's task in any culture is always to engage it without being engulfed by it . . . To achieve this biblical pattern of involvement – engaging our culture without compromising our faith – we must take two vital preparatory steps, both of which require us to listen rather than make premature pronouncements.' The first step that Steve advocates is to 'listen to the world' in order to understand the way in which culture works. The second is to '*reflect* on that culture, its values and direction, in the light of the Bible and its teaching.'

In other words, a Christian is not to stock up with Scripture verses as though these were hand-grenades to use against the world, and then to go out with a confrontational attitude and the Bible as a flak-jacket. Rather, the approach should be: first *listen*, then *reflect*. Don't go out looking for 'situations in which to quote Scripture', or you will find yourself using God's word inappropriately: 'Judas went out and hanged himself' (Matt. 27:5); 'Go and do likewise' (Luke 10:37).

The real world has many subtleties and nuances, in which it is easy to misapply the Bible through hasty judgment. Immediately lobbing a Bible quotation at someone is seldom the best way to develop a relationship, or to understand a situation. There are many Christians who need to pray, 'Lord, please help me to keep my big mouth shut until I know what I'm talking about!'

Instead, we need to *look* at problems; analyse them without judgment; and begin tentatively to *interact* with situations, in order to find out more information about the value systems of the various protagonists. Here's a recipe:

- Try to work out the underlying agendas.
- Then turn to the Bible to work out the ethics of the situation.
- See if there are people in the Bible who found themselves in similar moral dilemmas, and study the stance they took.
- Then begin prayerfully to *reflect* on all you have learned through this process.
- Once you are confident that you have accurately read the context, closely follow the Bible's teachings, as they apply to the moral and spiritual dimensions of the situation.

Phew! Now you're starting to understand and relate to modern culture, in a way that is fully Christian.

Imagine that you're sitting with a male colleague, who turns to you forlornly and says, with tears in his eyes: 'My boyfriend's left me. We've lived together for five years, but now he's gone off with some younger guy. I don't know how long it's been going on, but I'm worried that he might have infected me with the AIDS virus.'

Here's how NOT to respond: ' Well, you've only yourself to blame. The Bible clearly states in Leviticus eighteen verse twenty-two, do not lie with a man as one lies with a woman, that is detestable. Saint Paul says . . . Sodom and Gomorrah . . . eternal damnation . . . blah . . . blah . . . blah . . .'

The compassionate response is much simpler. It begins with the words: '*Do you want to talk about it?*'

Christian Distinctive

Some Christians will be getting very 'hot under the collar' at this point. This sounds a very New Age idea of transformation, without defining what it is that is being transformed, and into what? It can all seem to be very liberal. What, then, makes Community ministry or Christian Community development truly biblical? What distinguishes it from similar secular projects?

Well, in an AIDS context, for example, the defining factor is often that only a Christian project can truly hold out the hope of change. This change is sustainable through an underlying spiritual transformation. A person who is naturally promiscuous can be transformed by the Gospel message which enables the person to see the people with whom he or she is being promiscuous in a totally different light. Those who are at serious risk of HIV infection through sleeping around *can come to view members of the opposite sex as rounded people with importance and worth, and not simply as sex objects.* A person who comes to see that they are abusing both themselves and the people with whom they are being promiscuous can experience an astounding *spiritual transformation,* coming to see others as valued by God. The realisation then dawns that being promiscuous cheapens life, and that you leave behind something of your own identity – the most intimate aspects of your self-expression – if you constantly surrender to your lusts.

For those who are living in generational cycles of horrific sexual abuse and who are likely to start abusing their own children, the intervention of the Christian Gospel brings hope that the cycle can be broken. Relations with other people need not repeat the patterns of the past. We can combat the approaching spectre of alienation, by bridging the 'distances' between individuals with compassion, and rejoice that we are all part of God's great big family.

'Social change flows from individual actions,' says Robert Chambers in *Rural Development: Putting the Last First.*

By changing what they do, people move societies in new directions and themselves change. Big simple solutions are tempting but full of risks. For most outsiders, most of the time, the soundest and best way forward is through innumerable small steps and tiny pushes, putting the last first not only once but again and again. Many small reversals then support each other and together build up towards a greater movement.

The notion of the last being put first is, of course, a scriptural concept pertaining to the 'upside down' nature of God's Kingdom, where the humble are exalted, and the whole basis of social order is changed. Here, a person's life does not comprise the abundance of acquired possessions (Luke 12:15); anyone who stores up personal property is not rich in God's eyes (Luke 12:21); life is more than a set of commodities (Luke 12:23); but what you own and care about usually determines your values (Luke 12:34). 'Sell your possessions and give to the poor,' is a crux point in Christ's manifesto. 'Provide purses for yourselves that will not wear out, a treasure in heaven that will not be exhausted' (Luke 12:33). These values of generosity, self-denial and equality are the currency of God's Kingdom.

If a church *facilitates* the tantalising process of transformation, the church's profile changes amongst the people in the community, and the real issues come to the surface. Churches often ignore this approach because they are concerned only with seeing people come to make a Christian commitment. But if the person professes a faith without being given the opportunity to see how such faith can transform their everyday lives within their community, then the conversion is unlikely to last. They will not 'own' the conversion experience, because it will not be 'real' in their own terms, in their own lives. It will simply be an exercise they have carried out because it appears to be relevant to other people whom they want to please.

Through the Looking Glass

What do we actually mean by 'reflection'?

The *action-reflection approach*, put crudely, entails sitting down and analysing *what you have done*. When someone is cared for, or when someone is drawn into participation in a project or programme, there are many exciting ways to facilitate such reflection. The Church is littered with examples where reflection didn't take place when it should have done.

A prominent youth leader of a dying church eventually lost his patience. 'This place is going nowhere!' he barked. Shaking the dust from his feet, he stormed off. The man had lost his faith. Eight years on, the church was thriving under new leadership, with a community worker in place to develop a training workshop in the basement of the church premises. The backslidden youth leader – who was actually a carpenter by trade – was invited back to carry out some refurbishment to the building. Back in contact with his old church, he realised that much had changed; he was carried along by the dynamic ministry taking place within the church's walls, and he rediscovered his faith. During the action of being a joiner, the man had time and opportunity to reflect on 'what might have been'. *While the man was engaged in a purposeful activity with a useful Christian aim, he came to realise that there was a point to his life, and a destination in the far distance – which he could only reach by rededicating his life to Christ.* Here, it took a definite action – his recognition that the church had changed while he had been away from it – that spurred him to reflect on his values, and to begin a process of transformation. His understanding of the church had changed – and had changed the man with it.

Let's go back nearly two thousand years and meet a motley group of fishermen, following a charismatic religious leader. They admire him immensely, but they don't really understand the theology of the Kingdom of God that this man propounds. Perhaps he will turn out to be a great politician, or a prophet. Why, he might even turn out to be as important as Hosea, Zephaniah or Habakkuk! When Jesus puts these people directly in the firing line, on at least two occasions sending them out in twos to put the theory into practice, they gain a greater understanding.

'When the apostles returned, they reported to Jesus what they had done' (Luke 9:10). When they assess the events that befell them – reflecting on what has occurred – they learn still more.

'Then he took them with him and they withdrew by themselves . . .' (Luke 9:10). Jesus goes away from the crowds to try to be alone with his immediate band of followers. Later, in private, he asks them 'Who do you say I am?' (Luke 9:20). Soon, they are ready for Christ to take them deeper into the spiritual life, via the Transfiguration and a series of dramatic signs and wonders.

When their leader is crucified and rises from the dead, then here is an action which requires a very great deal of reflection! Jesus leads them in that reflection – taking them through the Scriptures and pointing out all the references to himself – and they eventually come to a complete understanding of their leader: specifically, they come to realise that he is God! Because they have had the experience – the action – of following him around for three years, their understanding of God is much fuller than if they had met the risen Lord without having known him before his death. Due to the greater depth of their understanding – because they have all the activities of his ministry upon which to reflect – they are better able to go out into the world and successfully preach the Gospel.

Mirror to the World

A church is often in an ideal position to help its surrounding community to reflect. One urban church bought a public house very cheaply from a brewery, who were pleased to be shot of it, because they were tired of paying out every time the premises were vandalised! The local people heard of this, and launched a petition to the local council to try to prevent the church from using the premises. The church had the opportunity to say to the community, 'Let us reflect on what *you* think church is really about, and what *we* think it is, in order that the pub can be put to a mutually agreeable use.' In a different situation, another church, Canning Town's Mayflower Family Centre, acquired an old pub specifically to use as a laundrette cum drop-in centre, with the upstairs part as a hostel – facilities that their research indicated were needed within the local community.

The *action-reflection* approach needs to become the Church's model for evangelism. People change by being given responsibility, and a classic example occurred all across Britain when the Christian charity Christmas Cracker asked young people from church youth groups to participate in setting up their own temporary radio stations, airing Christian music and talk. The experience completely changed those young people's understanding of what church was about: 'I thought church was "naff", but – wow! – running a radio station is really "cool"!'

The young people gained credibility with their peers, and some of the churches gained plausibility and acceptance in the community. While running the station, the young people had the opportunity to reflect: both on this exciting activity in which they were involved – which was raising money for projects in the Third World – and on how they *felt* about the whole experience. Countrywide, hundreds became Christians because they had been entrusted with responsibility – often for the first time in their lives – and they were thrilled to be projecting Christian values in such a hi-tech way. God had become relevant in their lives in a manner that had previously eluded them. They felt a keen sense of belonging, and realised that – in practice – the Gospel makes good sense.

Christmas Cracker changed local traders' perception of the Church. Local mini-cab firms began to put collecting tins in their cabs. Businesses sponsored particular programmes, or paid for spot advertisements. At its peak, over ninety stations per year went on air for several weeks in the run-up to Christmas, and several million pounds has been raised for charity projects that will bring liberation to some of the world's poor and needy people.

The Church has long been guilty of missing such opportunities. Christians have often believed that evangelism is about preaching the Gospel to people who come to church on Sunday, on the church's terms, and asking them to 'sign up' to a theory. It will only ever be a 'theory' to people until it becomes real in their lives, but – in the vicious circle – it will never become real to them while the Church continues to insist that participation in Christian work is only possible for those who have already 'bought into the theory'. God was pleased to use several pagan monarchs – Darius, Nebuchad-nezzar and Cyrus amongst them – in his plan for world redemption, but the Church has yet to accept that action can come before – or in spite of – the theory.

There is therefore a need for local churches to *re-formulate* and *re-assess* their underlying reasons for taking initiatives to transform local conditions which affect the lives of people. *Such reflection is the home of most excellent evangelism!*

Evangelism is really a process of introducing an alternative world view. It is the presentation of an apologetic that is radical, personal, and far-reaching. It is the place where hope, faith, change, new values, and – supremely – the person of Jesus Christ, are named as ingredients of a new and transforming lifestyle. Together, this approach is a dynamic model of action-reflection that fits with the model seen in the Gospels!

One church leafleted its area, not with tracts, but with invitations to come and help with the local elderly care programme. 'Come and do something you would actually like to do, and we will help you to reflect on it.' The volunteers are proud to identify with the work, their lifestyles have changed, and many have become Christians. Here is evangelism that is relevant and hard-hitting, with a keen cutting edge.

Agendas Revisited

There are many people across the globe who are struggling to free the poor from their chains of oppression, through such cutting-edge evangelism. Whether considering the global Church, an individual Christian, or a local congregation – in the affluent West or in the developing countries – the approach is very much the same.

Take Dr René Padilla for example. His country is Argentina, but his work could have happened anywhere, with the same results. The Kairos Community, which René heads up, is trying to examine the role of discipleship in today's world, and to help people to become involved in all kinds of action on behalf of the poor. They have a programme for training family counsellors, a theological programme aimed at professional people, and a community development programme.

Dr Padilla sees 'community' as simply 'a group of people who have something in common'. A *church* is a community that has a faith in Jesus Christ in common. The Kairos Community has a common cause, with which people work. It has a team that has developed programmes aimed at enabling individual churches to work with their own respective communities.

René says that a large percentage of the population have no access to the advantages that society offers, particularly in terms of education and healthcare. He yearns for a just society, but he doesn't expect it to become a reality in South America – where the situation is getting worse instead of better. His realistic hope is of small pockets of people that are living out the Gospel, where churches take responsibility for their surrounding communities.

There is a *cost* which deters many Christians from catching the vision. Time and money need to be invested in servanthood. René is not optimistic of making large-scale changes, but is seeing many small changes at grassroots level. He mentions a small project operated by a church in Buenos Aires, whereby local women can learn to generate income for their families. There are larger church-run projects, including a 'redemption project' which originated in a spiritually tepid Lutheran church, after the young people decided to go on to the streets and invite back some of the city's street children for a cup of soup. From this simple offer of friendship, they went further afield, and found their faith renewed in the process. The participatory process brought about change, not simply in the community, but in the church itself.

'It happens all the time,' says René:

In my own church, an educator in drug addiction was appointed to the pastoral team. We decided to teach about the nature and mission of the church through Bible expositions, but nothing much happened. Then we had an invasion of drug addicts –

about thirty of them – who began coming every Sunday, making a tremendous impact on the church. We had to begin to learn what it means to put into practice what we had previously only talked about! The whole programme of the church had to be restructured, and practical love had to be shown to the addicts, trying to find work for them. The whole life of the church was totally transformed. At first, some of the congregations were most unhappy with this, and I had to explain that the church is for *sinners*, and not for people who don't have any problems!

It was a wonderful experience. Now we are working with people with AIDS, and we have become a very loving church. It took some time. By God's grace, some people were prepared, but it was quite a process. In six months or so from the first addicts' arrival, this first person had become a staff worker on our ministry team. We paid him to go to the bars every night to find more addicts! The church has grown enormously as a result of this work. Twenty years have since passed, and most of the leaders are from amongst these former addicts. You would never guess that they had once been drug addicts.

These stories are common wherever churches are truly living out the Gospel. In the West, there is a church in Wales with 20 per cent of its congregation from amongst former drug addicts. Victory Outreach International has branches in Europe and America to reach out to former drug addicts, convicts and prostitutes, drawing 100 per cent of its congregations from these sources.

'In Latin America, we had an entire Christian culture with no ethics,' says René. The outward forms of religion were there, but there was no spiritual life, and no commitment to Christ. There was a good deal of corruption in political life, with exploitation of the poor, and abuse of power. The 'system' works for the rich and the powerful. You don't have to be a Marxist to realise that there are systems of oppression in this world that are organised to exploit the poor; a global economic system ruthlessly drains the resources of most Latin American countries.

God cries for Argentina. He doesn't keep his distance.

Reflections of Glasgow

John Matthews has reflected on his own work in Glasgow: 'Often when people have an encounter with the church, they go away bruised; they go away with a flea in their ear; they go away understanding that grace is costly,' says John, whose stories we heard in chapter two. When his parishioners approach him for 'rites of passage' – weddings, baptisms and funerals – he is aware that, if he makes too many demands, say, in terms of meetings to be attended before he will baptise a child, the parishioner will say, 'Bye-bye' and find a more liberal church. On the other hand, to 'baptise by hosepipe', bestowing wholesale sacrament whose meaning the parent has not taken the trouble to discover, is to lean too far into unorthodoxy. To achieve the level of engagement where such matters can even be discussed is not easy, John reflects, and his church's Tea Room is a useful bridge.

He has learned that it is one thing to read theology in the warmth of his study and quite another to put it into practice in a stressful pastoral situation:

Many evangelicals are theologically naive, because they don't *know* any lesbians; they don't *know* any homosexuals; they don't *know* any children who are born out of wedlock. The only way to understand, to speak and to inform in such situations, with your theology, is to encounter such people and to find out that they are delightful individuals – not stereotypes. In the process, you mustn't capitulate and say that the theology doesn't matter; nor must you be judgmental with a honed and polished theology that won't withstand practical application.

In the Bible, everyone but Christ makes mistakes! In today's world, Christians are petrified of making errors. Jesus was a risk-taker of the highest order, but the Church is terrified to emulate him in this willingness to take chances. Local congregations are afraid the world will gobble them up, or that they will compromise God's standards. But you won't read such attitudes in Scripture.

'We can't quite get the hang of loving God and loving our neighbour; most believers can manage one or the other. (Though 1 John 3:16–18 says it is *impossible* to love God without loving our neighbour.) Through their worship, Anglo-Catholics have learned to love God; and through their concern for social action, our liberal friends have managed to love their neighbours,' John says. But – like former US President Gerald Ford and his legendary inability to walk and chew gum at the same time – most of us are struggling to do two different things at once. Rather like being able to pat one's head and rub one's tummy at the same time, it takes practice! Understanding the humanity of Jesus is a helpful step. Our Lord wept at Lazarus's tomb. For him, this was not a 'photo-opportunity' or the occasion for a 'sound-bite' about being the resurrection and the life – it was a moment for human grief, and a time to identify with the often unbearable frailty and heaviness of being a mortal person. John Matthews says:

I know a married couple whose theology seemed to be set in concrete! Then, suddenly, their unmarried sixteen-year-old daughter became pregnant! Here was a piece of once-invariable theology transforming itself in front of them, as they were forced into reflection. They had passionately believed that the Church should *discipline* young Christians for such immorality – they should be barred from communion, and their church membership suspended until they regularised their relationship. But now, this was *their* daughter who was pregnant . . .

To see the change in this couple was interesting, to say the least. They were forced into reflection. They didn't compromise by adopting a less-stringent theology about sex-before-marriage, but they continued to love the girl and reconciled themselves to her mistake. From there, they came to realise that moral indiscretion and fall from grace can happen even to the most delightful of people, regardless of their home life and upbringing. What their daughter needed most was not discipline, but forgiveness and support.

Like Jesus Christ when his enemies brought to him a woman caught in the very act of adultery, this Christian couple did not adopt a judgmental attitude. They learned from Christ's treatment of this fallen woman; after exposing the hypocrisy of those who sought to condemn her, Christ suspended his own judgment, and asked the simple question, 'Where are your accusers?' – an enquiry to which he already knew the answer, but it served to open a dialogue with this unfortunate woman, dragged from her lover's bed, without making her feel even more uncomfortable.

Jesus did not give her the rollicking in private that he had been courteous enough not to give her in public; he simply told her to 'go and sin no more'. *As if she would!* She'd just learned her lesson the hard way, through the public humiliation to which she had been exposed, and from the risk of painful death by stoning – which would have been her probable fate had Christ not compassionately defused the situation. There was no point in Jesus labouring an exercise that the woman had already learned in the worst possible way. The demands of the law had been fulfilled – he had asked for accusers and no witnesses had come forward – now here was the moment for grace.

Perhaps churches across the world should pin notices on their doors: 'Drunkards, homosexuals, lesbians, criminals and junkies are all welcome here.'

Clay for the Potter

In the Tea Room, there is seldom any profound discussion of religious matters. People are most ready to speak about the brokenness of their own lives, and of their awful loneliness. Teenagers talk of the lack of affirmation and love they feel in their family. Betrayed women reflect on the pain their relationships have brought to them. Low self-esteem is common. They find the Tea Room a comfortable and secure place into which to bring their shattered lives. They may not want to talk about God at this point, but the stage is set so that when they experience a bereavement or a major personal crisis, there are Christian people available whom they have known for months or years, who will be there for them when they face their darkest hour.

They don't want to speak of *Spirituality* (with a capital 'S'), they want to talk about the aspect of their life where they feel the hurt, the peace, the thrill or the anger; the *emotions*. They may want to tell their story, and for someone to listen. Once this simple ministry has occurred, the situation might be advanced by asking, 'What can be done about the situation?' or 'How can I help?' in order to lead the person into reflection. The beginnings of an exploration of faith can often be teased from the answers. Yet people are free to leave whenever they like, which they can't in a church service – not without drawing attention to themselves.

The Church doesn't have too many tea rooms in which this gentle process of evangelism can take place, nor the 'stepping stones' to move the situation inexorably closer to the point of Christian commitment. Perhaps it has been too busy *speaking* to take the time to *listen* . . .

The creation of goodwill is a fine start. 'Being there' is important. John Matthews has had to keep asking his congregation to volunteer, but he now has twenty-three volunteers who are able to keep the Tea Room open five days a week. It's hard work, but the project has led to the complementary setting up of Alpha courses and exploratory Bible studies. And the Tea Room is only one strand in the church's work; there are Scripture Union clubs in local schools and a thriving youth club, all built on as units, to offer a wide range of 'attractions' sensibly supplying different opportunities for different people.

Through *reflection*, you begin to look at the familiar world in a different light. Then change can begin to take place. Once the reasons for doing nothing have been superseded, then the momentous process of transformation can commence. Sometimes – particularly in individuals – transformation conforms to the process that theologians call sanctification. But it isn't simply individuals that need to change, it is organisations and structures that need to be open to God and be willing to be lovingly re-moulded by the potter's skilful hand.

Questions

- Can you think of a situation in your own church where reflection might have been the most appropriate response to a difficult problem?
- How important do you think it is to have a good awareness of what other groups are doing in similar circumstances? Why?
- In what ways does your own church need to change?
- What would be the *cost* of such change, in terms of time needed, support required, and loss of control?
- If you were accused of being a practising Christian and put on trial, would there be enough evidence to convict you?

4

Partnerships

She's a pretty little thing, perhaps nine years old. Here in this grubby bar in Bangkok, she stands in a row with a dozen other girls scarcely older, each holding a card with a number on it. All scantily clad, they're circled by a small group of middle-aged Europeans who hover like a school of piranhas.

You watch, speechless, as one of the men bends close and runs his grubby hand over her young body. She trembles under his probing fingers. Your own flesh begins to creep.

Paralysed with disbelief, you see the man give a handful of dollars to the fat pimp and lead this young girl – she looks a bit like your niece – off towards a back room, his lips wet with drool. For a split second, the pre-pubescent nine-year-old turns and in an instant her eyes meet with yours. The child throws you a desperate look, pleading with sorrow behind moist eyes. This man is going to take her virginity.

Now! What are **YOU** going to do?

Are you going to be brave and rush in to save her? You'll get your head bashed in if you do; there are several rent-a-heavies standing around holding vicious wooden clubs! Call the police? It'll all be over before they arrive. If they do come at all, the pimp will simply pay them off with a back-hander.

Do you have enough money to do a deal with the pimp, and save the child? You'd better be quick!

But if you succeed in rescuing the girl from her immediate peril, then what next? Are you simply going to leave her for the next customer who comes along! Are you going to take her away somewhere? If so, can you afford to pay her pimp to release her? If you do, what will happen to her family, who need the money she will bring in to save them from starvation?

There is a strong probability that the girl's family will simply sell her younger sister's 'services' to the pimp. If you rescue this one child, what of the thousands of other child prostitutes who make Bangkok the world's sex capital? There are tens of millions of innocent victims who are forced to sell their bodies across the globe. By all means help this one girl – it's better to light one candle than to grumble about the darkness – but realise that this one incident is only the tip of an iceberg.

You're stuck! You've become a reluctant voyeur of a scene which unfolds millions of times each day, and there is no realistic way in which one individual can change the situation. Prostitution is part of a global black economy, making fortunes for people who always keep their own faces well hidden. Narcotics are a similar commodity, offering a chemical high that can blight a user's life as effectively as an illicit sexual kick with an HIV positive call girl. Both are dangerous, not simply for the consumer, but for everyone involved in the purveying of sleazy thrills.

Only committed individuals working together in *partnership* can begin to make a change. Local churches and para-church organisations – often working in collaboration with secular agencies, and even with governments – have a vital role to play in combating the degradation and affliction of these social ills. You're in the moral maze of law and order, where adequate remedies require electorates to pressurise their politicians to amend the legal framework within which societies function.

Sometimes the only adequate solutions have political dimensions (political with a small 'p', not party political) and – though welfare approaches will help in the short term – the developmental approach looks for sustainable political remedies. Politics is simply a way of explaining how people relate to one another in a society. The 'state' originated in a so-called social contract, whereby individuals accept a common superior power to make possible the satisfaction of certain human desires. Democratic governments have the delegated responsibility for the fair and effective regulation of society.

The only way, effectively, to put an end to child prostitution in Thailand – and in the Philippines, along with other parts of south-east Asia, Latin America and Africa – is through the co-operation of the various governments, and the police authorities that they control. But it's not just a problem for the developing world; to a lesser extent – though the girls are generally a few years older – prostitution remains a social curse even for the West. It's a global issue and the way forward isn't easy.

In the Lincoln Bedroom

In the West, we tend to look to politicians for moral leadership, often to find only sleaze and a sordid lack of personal ethics. In many developing countries, political instability has made many a Third World statesman concerned only about his own political survival, and the 'back-handers' which form his retirement plan. Whereas a European politician can generally be trusted to keep on the right side of the law in his or her financial propriety – even if those laws get a little bent sometimes – many of them savour distinctly unethical private lives.

Many countries of the world – particularly in Latin America and Africa – have been controlled by military juntas that shunned democratic control in the hands of the people. Often, dictatorships siphon away a country's assets into their own control – the now-deposed President Marcos of the Philippines, and President Noriega of Panama, are good examples. Many dictators have historically been kept in power by the CIA or the Kremlin. The year 1996–7 saw scandals and corruption allegations in Pakistan, India, Russia, China, Albania, Bosnia, Nigeria, Sierra Leone and many other countries.

Early 1997 witnessed a furore develop around the means that US President Bill Clinton had used to fund his re-election campaign the previous year. Foreign money to the tune of several million dollars mysteriously found its way into the Democratic national Committee's funds. Clinton was accused of illegally canvassing for donations on federal property. In particular, he seems to have favoured celebrity donors with overnight stays at the White House, allowing them to sleep in the Lincoln Bedroom – virtually a national shrine. Political cartoonists had a field day: one showed Clinton saying to a guest who was about to go to the toilet, 'Sorry, it's another $20,000 to use the washroom.' Don Imus, a New York talk show host, quipped that in the Lincoln Bedroom, 'You don't get a mint on the pillow, you leave one.'

In Britain, the 1990s saw a string of prominent politicians – including cabinet ministers – involved in sex scandals. Other MPs were implicated in a 'cash for questions' scam, whereby they were paid by commercial companies to acquire commercially useful information – under the guise of asking government departments for data, supposedly in connection with their constituencies. Greed and immorality stalk the corridors of power!

People need to take their citizenship seriously. Part of the empowerment process necessitates the building of confidence, in the poor and dispossessed, that they can bring about a difference politically – that their voice and their vote are important. The purging of local massage parlours and sex shops needs to take place simultaneously with the removal of immorality, corruption and sleaze from the political arena, through the ballot box.

Whether as genuine expressions of concern, or simply as means for politicians to remain in office, governing bodies are willing to work with community groups and development organisations the world over. Governments – be they local or national – can be 'won over' into participation in development programmes; indeed, they are often searching for development partners.

All the King's Men

Democracy, like Humpty Dumpty, may have taken a bit of a tumble, but there are still people in God's Kingdom who can nurse the West's ailing political system back to health. There are still men (and not enough women!) in politics with incorruptible hearts, and the moral courage to stand firm and take a stand against bribery and corruption. Many of them claim to be Christians, sitting in the British Parliament.

In the mid-nineties, Roy McCloughry interviewed a dozen British politicians for his book *Belief in Politics*. 'The family is the most basic building block of society, but the neighbourhood community also is crucial,' former Liberal Democrat MP David Alton told him. 'In the west of Ireland, where my mother comes from, they say of community that it's in the shelter of each other's lives that the people live.'

Labour Prime Minister Tony Blair agreed with Alton's emphasis on community: 'Where my political and personal beliefs completely coincide is in the notion that people are members of the community and society, not simply individuals, isolated and alone.' For Blair, the role of the individual in society is a 'distinguishing feature of the Christian religion'. These same broad values are shared by former Conservative minister Peter Lilley, who says: 'There's no doubt that the assistance one person can give a neighbour directly counts more than a similar amount given through the rather anonymous structures of the state.'

These Christian MPs, then – like others that McCloughry interviewed – hold views on the importance of community that by-pass party politics. As McCloughry himself says, 'The word "community" represents a new emphasis on "belonging" as a characteristic of human relations. . . . [It] is now seen as an important new resource in politics.' He reflects on the needs for a transforming agenda, a new vision, and – as the party political messages merge – greater choice.

Alan Haworth, a former Conservative politician who crossed the floor of the house in disgust at widening inequalities and neglect of public services, said: 'If neighbours are strangers, truly there is no such thing as society', such is the crucial importance of community life. The Home Secretary, Jack Straw, has suggested that the power of the community can be used to advance the interests of the individual and the family, with markets as the *servants* of the community; and Simon Hughes MP agrees that bottom-up models are preferable to solutions that are prescribed from the top down. Community development will dominate the political agenda well into the next century, with its keen emphasis on consultation and partnership.

The major problem for any British government for the foreseeable future will be to address the scandal of unemployment – a problem that is unlikely to resolve itself naturally. Charities – particularly those working in community development – are crying out for helpers, and it remains to be seen whether the current Labour government's welfare–to–work policy will draft the unemployed into quality jobs that will help to bring about positive change in communities at home and abroad.

The Church's contribution to the solution would appear to lie in mobilising Britain's church members. The UK Christian Handbook gives a figure of over 6,500,000 UK Christians in 1990, projected to fall by around three-quarters of a million by the year 2000. People may not have given up on God, but they are giving up on the Church! Of these 750,000, many are nominal members, and it may be that *the decline is due to church members feeling unused and undervalued within their congregations.* The Evangelical Alliance estimates a figure of around 1,000,000 committed evangelicals in the UK, and the number is steadily growing. There is potentially a mighty army available to work alongside any government initiatives in community transformation. But is it realistic to expect such help, when most Christians still seem to be *frightened* of politics? There are serious problems.

An Oppressive Church

Let's be painfully blunt about this.

The Western church is largely middle-class and elitist. Working-class people are generally far less likely to be invited to participate in leadership roles than those in 'good jobs'. Perhaps most draconian is the first- and second-class Christian divide, created by the ordination of 'priests' and ministers. Christ had little complimentary to say about the priests of his own day, and it is difficult to believe that he actually intended to create a separate priesthood in any way distinct from the one to which all believers belong, and of which they become members through conversion. This is not to diminish the reality and weighty responsibilities of leadership roles given by God within the Church, but it is intended to challenge the perception that some are 'six feet above contradiction'. The Old Testament pattern of priesthood saw priests as intercessors on behalf of the whole Jewish people. As the New Testament priesthood of all believers take their prayer life seriously, they take on that full Old Testament role of intercession for the world.

Some have argued that the refusal to have women ordained as priests is, then, not simply a weapon of oppression directed against the women, but a red herring distracting from the priesthood of all believers – the only priesthood which matters – and a travesty of a Gospel which welcomes everyone regardless of colour, gender or background. Unless the Church is prepared to change, it seems likely that Christianity as a faith will continue its decline the West.

Christ communicated largely through innovative story-telling that was centred around strong images from everyday life – the sower, the mustard seed, weeds, hidden treasure, pearls, and the like. Some modern preachers often communicate oppressively, like headmasters addressing a school assembly. In their pulpits, six feet above contradiction, they sometimes seem determined to get to the end of their three-point sermon, even when their text does not suit such an approach. There is seldom the opportunity for a congregation to give collective feedback or to enter into dialogue about the sermon. Opportunities to use video, slides, drama, dance and illustrations are seldom used as preaching tools in most churches – though the late David Watson used them extensively, and they are used effectively in a number of urban churches, where adult literacy rates are relatively low.

Getting out on to the streets of a community as Jesus did, meeting people and relating to their needs, is assigned a low priority, or reserved for 'the experts' – the vicar or elders. Coffee mornings, prayer meetings and church parties need to be complemented by the housing action, welfare advice work, day centres for the elderly, creches for single parent families, and concern for social justice which are on God's agenda, but which are tackled currently by only a few people at denomination headquarters. There is tremendous scope for improvement. Once you begin to look below the surface veneer, you begin to find that most Christians are deeply *frustrated*. They are simply not given the opportunities to develop proper ministries of their own.

'Giving your life to Christ' surely means letting Christ work through you to achieve his objectives – which include helping the poor, *not* oppressing them. We affirm the truth of salvation by grace through faith, but believe that faith means more than simply an intellectual acceptance of a set of beliefs. Christians trust, not in those beliefs, but in the person of Christ as he is active within their lives by the power of the Holy Spirit. *If he is not active in our lives in a similar way to the Gospel pattern, then we ought to be suspicious as to whether the spirit of Christ is really at work within us.*

Christian activist Jim Wallis suggests that the Church worldwide might be ripe for a 'Second Reformation' whose primary paradigm would be the Church as 'a Church for the Poor', with values and programmes similar to those which are suggested here. Perhaps Wallis is premature. It's not a new reformation that we require, but the completion of the old. Luther's reforms began to end some of the long oppression by the Church, under which the people of his day suffered. *Christians will only reach the unchurched by becoming more 'user-friendly' at their points of contact with a hurting world; by completing the reforms which many are seeking to make within our structures; and by repenting of the institutionalised sin which is corroding the face of Christ which the world sees in the Church.*

Changing the Church may *seem* a bit like reinventing the wheel; but it's probably more accurate to say that the wheel fell off, and no one has put it back on recently . . .

Sometimes the future looks bleak, and it can appear that the Church really won't change in a month of Sundays; but there is hope. There are many Christian pioneers whose work is often overlooked. Just as there are good people in the corrupt world of politics, so there are many in the Church who are committed to change, and who desire to see local churches become the beacons of God's Kingdom.

Partners in Enablement

The congregation of St John's, Bascombe, set up a playgroup to meet a special need in the heart of their community. Derek Baldwin, in *Open Doors, Open Minds*, comments:

> From the outset it was made clear that the group was run on Christian principles and the children would be told about God's love for them in Jesus. Parents seemed to accept this without demur. Indeed, they often ask Julie [the playgroup leader] or her helpers questions about Christian things – ostensibly for their children but actually because for some it is on this level they can take it in for themselves. Some, having become used to bringing their child to the Centre, seem willing to do so on Sunday mornings. A few of the parents may then stay for all-age worship themselves, provided that one of the helpers or Christian parents they have got to know during the week sits with them. Some have found faith this way.

Though this scheme adopted a *welfare* approach rather than a true *development* approach, most churches would have been content to stop at that point and to rest on their laurels. Instead, St John's next took the consultative step of *listening* to discover the community's own agenda, making good use of questionnaires. When local people were asked: 'Do you practise a religion?' one replied, 'My wife's a Christian, but I'm more a beer and skittles man myself'!

Through *reflection*, the church began to discern and respond to a call to servanthood. It began to call itself the Church of the Open Door, and set about transforming its local community, in *partnership* with the local people. It broke down barriers and literally became transparent by replacing its sturdy wooden doors with glass doors so that passers-by could see inside. A drop-in centre attracted a range of needy people whose chief need was for simple friendship. 'First we must take the trouble to understand their need and reach them at that point,' says Baldwin in his book. 'The concept of "earning" the right to *speak* to people about the love of God by first *showing* them his love in action is a familiar one.' His church continues to display God's unconditional *agape* love, even in the face of setbacks and disappointments, and it has soon moved on to develop a church for the unchurched – drawing on principles that we will be considering later on.

Another church discovered that bullying was becoming a problem at their local school. Their investigations revealed that the head-mistress was a Christian and only too pleased to support an initiative to resolve the problem. A course ran during the lunch hour to bring bullies and their victims face-to-face. Games enable the children to get to know and understand each other better and to build good behaviour. Timid children are encouraged to be more assertive, while the bullies learn to see how unkind they have been. This project was only possible through the *partnership* between school and church, the secular and religious authorities. Where necessary, parents are also brought into the fruitful partnership.

The agenda for many evangelical Christian leaders, and organisa-tions such as Tear Fund and the Evangelical Alliance, for the next ten years is beginning to include the importance of facilitating such participation by Christians in their local communities. Practical strategies for local action by local Christians are being developed by UK Action project partners. These can, with proper adaptation, be replicated elsewhere. There is also a need to explore how non-believing and agnostic people can be drawn into the Church's agenda for community development as a means of bringing the transforming influence of Jesus Christ to bear to their lives.

Partners in Ownership

The first principle of Christian community development is *maximum ownership* by all concerned. Ownership equates with hours given to local initiatives. Ownership results in change through participation. Any expression of the caring Church that reduces the practical contact between the person in the street and the person in the pew totally misses the point. Any initiative which marginalises the practical involvement of ordinary Christians will repeat the unsatisfactory history of the Church in its mission to transform and be transformed.

To make change in people's lives, there has to be spiritual change – that is how you change the way people see themselves, see others, and see God. Transformation is primarily about making people look at the world in a different way. For example:

A church in a Kampala slum trained up twenty local volunteers to provide basic care to people with HIV. One man declared that he was dying of AIDS, 'and damn it, I'm going to infect as many people as possible before I die'. Life had dealt him a bitter blow, and he wanted to deal one back in retaliation. Christian volunteers began to visit the man, taking food, cleaning his house, and cleaning him up. Eventually the man started reflecting. He began to wonder why these people were so kind to him: 'My neighbours don't want to know me, so why are you doing this for me?' The volunteers explained that God cared for him, and so did they. Eventually he started turning up at the church. When asked what had happened to bring about the change in his life, he replied, 'Because you started treating me differently, it made me think that I must have some value. If I have value to the point where you will come and look after me, perhaps the people with whom I have been promiscuous have value too, which I should acknowledge and not abuse. If there is a God, I want to know him.' The man became a Christian before he died.

This is a good Third World lesson that can be applied in the West – though Tear Fund has discovered that its overseas partners are often much more ready to try community participation than the average Western church! Christian development agencies like Tear Fund try to respond to someone else's agenda, but only an agenda that a church should have anyway.

Tear Fund's UK Action initiative says, 'You come to us with your agenda, and we will see if we can help to build your capacity to fulfil that agenda.' Building up capacity entails training, a certain amount of funding (though if there is money involved, it is not an *equal* partnership), visits to other projects, and developing a vision. Visiting other projects often challenges the way in which people think about how to do something. If there is a different way of achieving the same ends without such heavy dependency on outside funding, then UK Action will try to find it.

Partnerships are about *enablement*. If the poor are viewed as passive victims of an unfair world, they will end up feeling patronised and sceptical. They will also imbibe a 'victim' mentality. Consequently, their sense of dependency will be deepened, and the Gospel message will not be well received. If, however, the poor are seen as people who are capable of taking an initiative, and changing from dependency into active and contributing members of the community, then the good news of Jesus will be received more wholeheartedly.

Finding a good *part*ner is a *part* of the process of change. To make such change sustainable involves *participation* in spiritual transformation, because it demands that people see one another in a new way.

How do you make partnerships work? The attitude of the partners is vital, and their respect for one another is essential. There is always friction, teething trouble, and an energy input that is needed to maintain partnerships. If the benefit is huge, then it outweighs this cost; if the benefit is very small, then perhaps there is little point in keeping together a partnership of people who might do better if the partnership is broken. It all seems like a good recipe for a personal relationship, as much as a development enterprise!

Christmas Cracker's chairman, Ram Gidoomal, reflects:

In practice, the one who puts in the money always seems to dominate, with a neo-colonialism that says 'I've got the money, and therefore I have the main say.' With Christmas Cracker, I was the one who brought in the sponsors and therefore the money, but I refused to remain part of the executive. As in the business world, I always used to delegate responsibility, and to allow others to take decisions. As in commerce, if I was paying them a fortune for their experience, I was going to make sure that I drew out their expertise and core competency!

Cracking Talents

Ram Gidoomal was visiting Mumbai (or Bombay as it was then called) and being shown around a slum by Christian community workers, before catching his plane back to Britain. When Ram asked what *he* could do to help with the terrible poverty he witnessed, the workers told him what *they* were already doing. They didn't dictate an agenda to Ram, but they allowed him to try to find a way to participate in the one that they were already following themselves, which their local community had set for them. *There was an opportunity here for Western Christians to become development partners, and to lift the fear of debt from the shoulders of these Christians in their important and inspiring work.* The way these church workers operated together as partners set Ram's agile mind racing:

These people proceeded to explain that though they were from different denominations and different churches, they had only one photocopier between them. My goodness! I realised that, in Britain, ten different churches would have ten different buildings and ten different photocopiers; but here, where resources were tight, they had to share in a way which ensured that a little went a long way. *Here was true partnership in mission.* They had realised that the only way forward was to learn how to tolerate and to share with each other.

When Ram began to work with Steve Chalke in founding the Christmas Cracker charity initiative, the first thing Ram arranged was for all the mission agencies from which they needed to attract support to come together in the same place at the same time. Around twenty mission agencies showed up at a London church, for a wonderful meeting.

'Lesson number one,' says Ram, 'is don't organise twenty meetings with twenty different people; organise one meeting to which twenty people come!' A week's work was saved through this simple expediency which Ram had been taught in a Third World situation. The poor Indian church had given back something important to the rich British church.

At the meeting itself, Ram employed another lesson learned from the Mumbai slums. He explained that he wasn't interested in setting up yet another mission agency, with its own agenda. He wanted to serve the agendas of those that already existed, and to channel the money raised from dynamic fund-raising initiatives via those existing agencies. Tear Fund were the first to respond with a small gift, followed by a loan from Interserve, and a series of other small gifts from other agencies. Like Christ's parable of the talents, Christmas Cracker was given the seed money, which it then began to multiply rapidly.

The charity utilised Oasis Trust's core competency in working with young people, and began to share this with the wider Christian community. Within a year, half a million pounds had been raised by the efforts of Christian young people across Britain, who found themselves in a position of trust and responsibility, with a real job to do within their churches – many for the first time. Simple lessons learned from a slum work in Mumbai paid rich dividends: £4,000,000 in the first seven years, utilising the talents of an estimated 50,000 young people working together in partnership.

In the 1980s, the business world placed emphasis on *structures*, but the 1990s saw the emphasis move from structures to *people*, with a strong relational emphasis: 'Relational management, and people working together with a high value on the worth of individuals, has been the liberating experience. Instead of fitting into a mould, we worked in a way that was best for the situation. We took the most cost-effective, and people-effective, methods to maximise the impact,' says Ram, and Christians would do well to apply these principles in their own local situations.

Partners in Change

When Comic Relief, a group of comedians and broadcasters running a telethon, began working in partnership with development agencies, they didn't just raise the money and give it away – they took great care to ensure that it was used wisely. Comedian Lenny Henry visited homelessness projects to see how the money was being spent. A group of entertainers formed a football team playing friendly matches with African village teams, in order to get to know the people they were helping, and to understand their problems at first hand. When comedian Billy Connolly first visited Mozambique, he was told by an agriculturist, 'we don't want gifts, we want agricultural tools'. When Connolly revisited seven years later, those agricultural implements had been put to good use.

A classic development partnership is the one between the journalists who produce the weekly general-interest magazine *Big Issue*, and the homeless vendors who sell it on the streets. Here, homeless people are empowered by being given a commercial product that they can sell and retain a significant slice of the cover price. They maintain their dignity through the legitimate income that is generated, which makes them less dependent on begging or state handouts. The regular contact between vendors and customers helps the homeless people to find their way back into society; eases their way back into employment; and provides a sense of purpose. The idea has proved to be so successful that various editions of the *Big*

Issue are now produced in many cities in the UK and abroad.

Both of the above initiatives were taken by non-Christians. Sometimes it can seem that the non-Christians have got it all 'sussed' well ahead of the Church, but there are Christian agencies who have long been 'on the ball' as far as effective development work is concerned.

Tear Fund has been at work in the Philippines since 1985, working with its development partner PHILRADS to help the 2,000 squatters who for many years regarded Manila's Smokey Mountain rubbish tip as their home. Families on Smokey Mountain had traditionally eked out a meagre living by sifting through unsafe mountains of rubbish scavenging for items to recycle and sell. Initially, healthcare, education, sewage disposal, vocational training, fresh water and spiritual witness were provided. Then, when the government resettled the people in apartments, PHILRADS set up a clinic for them. 'The people have somewhere to live now,' says Tear Fund General Director Doug Balfour, 'but no source of income.'

Many young Filipinas have now been forced to work the streets, where the average age of a prostitute is fourteen. Poverty is often responsible for the debauchery and immorality which serve as an escape from an unpalatable reality, and casual sex with a prostitute is treated by the punters as a panacea for the pain, insecurity and anguish of everyday life in an impossible situation. As for the girls, can we really condemn a fourteen-year-old for what she is doing? How can we try to facilitate a change in her life? *What is the role of the Church in this situation?* It is certainly not 'tutting', or doing evangelism in the normal way. But *care* is highly evangelistic, because it leads to change. Local Christians are reflecting on the situation, while struggling to help the poor and displaced people to cope with life in a more positive way. Doug Balfour explains:

Our overseas partners have learned how to connect into the local community, and they have been able to mobilise the community whilst still being a part of it, without losing sight of the goal of *spiritual* transformation as well as social transformation. I have seen it in Honduras with the Miskito Indians, where there is a tremendous work with land rights and conservation issues. In Uganda, there is an AIDS project working on similar lines. In the Bible, Christ says that when they see the good works you do, they will give praise to your father (Matt. 5:16) and it's very true that people know a good thing when they see it. The Gospel makes excellent sense in terms of 'bottom-up' community development strategy.

The confidence that people should have in the Gospel is the same confidence that they have when they put salt into their frozen peas that the peas are going to come out tasty; or that when you put yeast into bread, it is going to rise.

Companion to the Poor

New Zealander Viv Grigg is one man who sought to live out the Christian Gospel amongst Asia's urban poor. He has tried to avoid the unhelpful separation of people's spiritual needs from their physical. Viv believes that Christians are called to disciple the nations, and that the discipling process involves dealing with a person's environment, as well as his or her personality. In his book *Companion to the Poor*, Viv reflects on the costly sacrifices that are entailed, and says that 'in maintaining a commitment to righteousness and social justice in the context of legalised oppression and exploitation, we may at times have to be aligned with particular political groups. But such a commitment will be primarily pastoral. Ultimately we have no political ideology except that of the justice and righteousness of the Kingdom of God – a stance which, in practice, is not apolitical.'

The authentic search for the historical Jesus inevitably leads deep into the dark heart of poverty, for Christ is most fully present at the point of deepest need. 'Where there is suffering, he will be there binding wounds. His compassion eternally drives him to human need,' says Viv. 'Where there is injustice, he is there. He does not dwell on the edge of the issues. He is involved, always doing battle with the fiercest of the forces of evil and darkness.' These spiritual forces are not sword and sorcery characters from a Frank Peretti novel, but the reality of injustice and oppression.

Viv reflects that individual Christians and childless couples can generally live effectively amongst the urban poor, so long as they have: a good toilet; decent cooking facilities; a day of rest outside the slums each week; and a reliable companion. The notion that Christianity is purely a private spiritual matter between each individual and God is soon shattered by ministry there, where care-evangelism soon demands social, economic and political dimensions.

True discipleship is caught, not taught. 'It is not a method, a program, nor even the teaching and preaching of the word of God – though all of these are involved. *Disciplemaking is God's love being poured out through one life into another, until the second life catches that love,*' Viv argues passionately.

Being a channel for God's divine love demands the surrender of private ambition and personal vanity. Like Christ – who did not count equality with God as something to be grasped, but took the form of a servant and humbled himself, even to death on a cross – you must lose all vestige of pride, loftiness and self-seeking, to truly become God's warrior in the war of love. Only *then* is God able to use you to draw others to himself through your sacrificial ministry. Expect nothing in return except for God's endorsement as his good and faithful servant, and Christ's promise:

Come and take your inheritance, the kingdom prepared for you since the creation of the world. For I was hungry and you gave me something to eat, I was thirsty and you gave me something to drink, I was a stranger and you invited me in, I needed clothes and you clothed me, I was sick and you looked after me, I was in prison and you came to visit me . . . I tell you the truth, whatever you did for the least of these brothers of mine, you did for me. (Matt. 25:34–6, 40).

The measure of effective partnership is reflected in the words of an old Chinese poem:

> Go to the people,
> Live among them.
> Learn from them.
> Start with what they know.
> Build on what they have;
> But of the best of leaders,
> When their task is accomplished,
> Their work is done,
> The people all remark
> 'We have done it ourselves.'
> (Lao Tsu, 700 BC)

Questions and Exercises

- How can churches be made more friendly and welcoming?
- Are there any examples of sexist behaviour, or any other form of discrimination, in your own church? Think of the best way of bringing this tactfully to the attention of the leaders.
- Re-read the story of St John's, Boscombe. What implication does this work have for your own church?
- Do you agree with Viv Griggs? Give reasons for your answer.
- Try to find someone in your own church who would partner you in a development project in your own locality. (At this stage, you only need their help and support *in principle*.)

5

Cry Freedom!

British-born Martin Neil makes his living as a hit man! He is a professional drummer, who has played on albums by many leading Christian artists, including Phil and John, Martyn Joseph, Graham Kendrick and Kevin Prosch. He has toured the world as a musician in various ministry teams, and he has seen many different forms of poverty at first hand. When he is not giving his drums some stick, he has taken the opportunity to get alongside the poor and deprived people that he has met on his travels.

In 1992, Martin went out to St Petersburg to take part in the first ever multi-cultural Christian arts festival to be held in Russia. On the city streets, he witnessed queues for basic necessities – bread and milk – stretched around the block. In all the stores the shelves were empty, but the Christian people whom Martin met, and who joyfully invited him into their homes, managed to provide tea and biscuits. The young people growing up in the wake of glasnost had clear ambitions regarding their future careers. All the young men wanted to join the Mafia, and all the young women wanted to be prostitutes, because these were the only occupations

85

that offered decent potential to make an indecent living! These careers offered their last and best hope of building a future for themselves. 'Yet I heard sad stories of prostitutes being beaten by their pimps. It was a regular occurrence,' Martin laments.

Banging his Drum for the Poor

On another visit, this time to Nigeria, it seemed to Martin that everyone believed in God – and such was the deplorable standard of driving, it often looked as though road users were going to meet him sooner, rather than later! Martin says:

Ask them why they overtook in spite of oncoming traffic, and they will say, 'God is with us'. There is a spiritual side to their life, but it is quite fatalistic.

Within the first twelve hours of arriving in the country, we had officials trying to extort as much money out of us as possible at the airport, and then bandits attempted to hi-jack us on the motorway! All the accommodation is one-storey, and when it rains all the houses and roads flood. The water is undrinkable, without getting seriously ill; and it's dangerous to walk the streets alone. When one Christian took me to his village home, all his neighbours came running up to touch me, because they had never seen a white person before.

On another occasion, a colleague nearly started a riot when he tried to shoot some video footage; the Muslim population don't like it, because they think the camera will steal their souls. They were throwing punches through our car windows. If you don't understand the different cultures, you're soon going to be in trouble.

Nigeria has many picture postcard scenes, and a casual visitor could easily miss the shanty towns and slums. As in many African countries, there is great inequality and injustice, with one law for the rich and another for the poor. In other countries, it isn't just drum skins that get beaten with sticks. One traveller, Gordon Barley, has commented in the book *The Long Way Home*:

> In tropical Zaire, two of my companions had their money stolen by a sneak thief who cut open the canvas of their tent to relieve them of their valuables. The matter was reported to the local police, who dragged off one of the local young people into a nearby mud hut, where we heard his terrified screams as he was beaten. We believed that the African police had found a scapegoat and thrashed him, virtually torturing him, in order not to lose face in front of us Europeans. The politics of many of those African countries was way 'off the wall'; they were virtually police states.

Martin Neil's own travels have taken him out into the Pacific Ocean to the Philippines:

> I've never smelt anything so horrendous in my life as the Smokey Mountain rubbish tip, which ten thousand families called home. The torrential monsoon rains made Smokey Mountain into a death trap when the rubbish began to move because of the water pressure. One church pastor lived incarnationally, getting alongside the community by living on the rubbish heap himself. The rich estates were patrolled by guards, as the wealthy took precautions to hang on to their prosperity; and these rich enclaves would often be right next to the slum areas.

In Malaysia, Martin noticed a great contrast in the religious life: 'Whereas in the Philippines, there were many large churches and a sense of hope in the area, in Malaysia, there seemed to be less poverty, but also an absence of large churches and very little sign of hope. *In a way, I think you have to be poor to have hope.* Wherever I have met poverty, I have found a great willingness on the part of the people to hear about Christ.'

In his epochal book *Rich Christians in an Age of Hunger*, Ronald Sider pulls no punches when he writes: 'It is a sinful abomination for one part of the world's Christians living in the Northern Hemisphere to grow richer year by year while our brothers and sisters in the Third World ache and suffer for lack of minimum healthcare, minimum education, and even – in some cases – just enough food to escape starvation.'

Beaten Skin: Poverty in the West

For Martin, visiting Albania was like going back 150 years. In 1992, there were only a handful of private cars in the whole country; now there are white Mercedes cars out there carrying gentry through the countryside. The change has been very rapid, and the people can't adjust to it; most of them are still humble peasants cultivating their land. During the communist era anyone who dropped litter was fined; now everybody throws everything everywhere! For fifty years, they had been told the lie that they were surrounded by the Western world, wanting to invade Albania to steal its prosperity.

Martin was particularly struck by the poverty he saw in the United States:

You can live your whole life there, not knowing that there *is* poverty, because it is largely restricted to the inner cities, while the well-to-do live in the suburbs. When I was visiting Seattle, I decided to get up early in the morning and explore the city. I was absolutely shocked by what I saw! I'd seen Third World conditions, but to see such similar conditions in a country considered to be a land of opportunity was devastating. There were people lying by the side of the road begging. There were ghettos and 'no-go areas' of a severity I have never seen in the UK; indeed, Nigeria is the only other country where I've seen such dangerous places, where casual visitors are likely to get a serious beating.

Injustice stalks the streets of the USA, where the poorest one-fifth of the population receive 4 per cent of the nation's income per year, while the richest one-fifth garner a whopping 44 per cent. (Source:

Centre for Budget and Policy Priorities, 1990.) 'In the USA the federal authorities started a war on poverty,' writes Alf Ronnby in *Mobilising Local Communities*. 'The participation of the ghetto population was seen as one of the ways of beating their apathy and sense of emptiness. It was stressed that poverty was not so much a question of the lack of material resources but a lack of power.'

Ronald Sider gives a Christian perspective, emphasising that power and prosperity do not bring happiness:

Millions of North Americans and Western Europeans are in despair as they seek in vain for happiness through ever greater material abundance. The idolatrous materialism of the economic rat race creates alcoholics, ruined marriages and heart attacks. Jesus offered a better way through sharing. We cannot gain happiness by seeking it directly. It comes as a by-product as we give ourselves to others.

Britain's streets, too, are no strangers to poverty. 'Though I see so much good work happening around the world that is all well and good, there is much that needs to be done on my own doorstep, in London,' says Martin Neil, who is glad to bang his drum about ASLAN (a project run from All Souls Church, Langham Place) which operates a tea-run for the homeless:

One time, we were out in the early morning and we came across three children on the streets, who had just run away from home in Coventry. They were around fifteen years old, and this was their first night sleeping on the streets. We put them in our van and took them up to Centrepoint Soho, a secular resettlement agency, where they were given help. I was very moved by the experience.

Many homeless young people are quickly drawn into prostitution and drug dependency, so Martin gave thanks to God that he was able to meet these people before they fell into the hands of pimps and pushers.

One thing I've learned through ASLAN is that, if you have a lot of people each doing a little bit, then you can get a lot done. It's surprising how little effort is required, if everyone joins in. But many Christians don't realise the difference they can make. Others would be very willing to help if there was something for them to do, but I don't think there are enough visionary people putting projects together in which Christians can get involved. You would think the Church would have learned that a lot of people, each doing a little, can change the world. It all starts by people saying, 'Let's do something!' each being prepared to try to play their part in freeing people from poverty.

The only thing that I have done is to *be available*. There are still lots of aspects of the work that quite scare me. I've never slept on the streets myself, so I know I can't really *identify* with those who do, and that's the scariest thing; but I know that I can try my best.

Martin was prepared to play his part in helping people to stage a jailbreak, out of the poverty trap. But others are adept at devising elaborate excuses to disguise their apathy. Here are some typical excuses: 'I don't know enough about the situation'; 'If I do something, it might make me unpopular'; 'I'm afraid of what might happen'; 'I have more important things to do'; and 'It's not my job'.

The Poverty Culture

Poverty takes many forms, of which lack of choice, injustice and oppression are often the most manifest symptoms. 'But it is more than economic,' complained single parent Maria Jones in *The Independent* (7/8/96). 'Low-income families, children in care, and the elderly in homes are all treated by the state as though we are not quite human. Have you any idea what it is like to have a social worker going through your cupboards to see what you've bought and whether it meets their standards of priorities?' Poverty is about being isolated and unwanted; living with other people's wallpaper;

buying all your clothing second-hand; and having to borrow from loan sharks because banks think you're a poor risk. 'How can you teach table manners to children who live in a house so small that there's no room for a dining table?'

Poverty insinuates its way into many areas of life, as David Evans found when his work took him from a leafy suburb to a poor inner-city area. In moving from comfortable Hertfordshire, a rural idyll, to Bermondsey in inner London, David became aware that he was crossing innumerable cultural boundaries. These were reflected in the contrasting nature of church life. In the Hertfordshire context, the character of the church resonated with the nature of the town, with a sense of independence and cultural success, where people were anxious to talk about their successes and to conceal their failures.

There was a lack of material need, generally a smooth veneer of respectability threatened to cover any breakdown of relationships, and difficulties were not confronted. Churches in this kind of suburban situation, despite genuine faith, sometimes find it difficult to connect with the outside world. This church created its own inward-looking agenda – one of *religious consumerism* – and chose not to face up to real issues. There was a lack of vision for the local community, other than as a hunting ground for new evangelistic 'scalps'. Instead, twenty-minute arguments might ensue in church meetings over such monumental decisions as, 'What colour should we choose for the new pedal bin' . . .

When David and his family moved a mere forty-five miles to Bermondsey, it was like moving to another continent! Instead of a lack of material need, they had to confront an enormous material deprivation. The veneer of respectability was cracked and peeling, failures were acknowledged, and people wore their hearts on their sleeves. People said what they meant, often speaking with their fists. Instead of success, there was only a debilitating burden of cultural failure. A dependency culture thrived, with people transferring themselves into dependency on the church, which found itself in a welfare mode very quickly. *The culture shock was as severe as moving overseas.*

Churches often create an insular sub-culture, and structures that keep the world at arm's length, as a protection against reality – instead of a springboard for releasing people into the community. In attempting to throw out worldly things, we actually throw the world out!

There was an enormous measure of vision, but no sense of stability to sustain any new initiatives; and too many options, most of which led nowhere. David's new church only wised up to the fact that it needed to become more developmental after it had burned out a couple of church workers.

We tend to judge how well a church is developing by the way *we* feel about it, rather than how *God* feels about it! A spot of invigorating worship and a bracing sermon and we tend to think that all is well with the Church – but our own emotions are a faulty guide. It's all very well to be up praying till four in the morning, but if the quality of our prayer life does not reflect into our practical walk with God and imbue our loving concern for others, then we are in spiritual poverty. St Paul certainly felt that way: 'If I speak in the tongues of men and of angels, but have not love, I am only a . . . clanging cymbal . . . If I give all I possess to the poor and surrender my body to the flames, but have not love, I gain nothing' (1 Cor. 13:1, 2).

Many Christians don't have the full riches of Christ. We have only the foretaste and we confuse the mouthful with the full meal; we mistake the symbol for the reality. We think we've eaten a hearty spiritual meal, when actually we are Christian consumers treating the Christian life as a string of commodities, and we have disgraced ourselves by noisily slurping up the finger bowl!

The time has come for re-evaluation. The Church needs to 're-examine its long-standing reliance on large-scale institutional or professional solutions to human needs', advocates Tom Sine in *The Mustard Seed Conspiracy*. 'Let's ask whether our institutional / professional systems are really promoting God's agenda in solving problems and bringing change within the Church and the society or merely perpetuating an expansive service bureaucracy.'

To move from the form to the reality, the Church needs to begin a process of change.

In *The Upside-down Kingdom*, Donald Kraybill writes:

The Church is always caught in the tension between the traditional solutions of the past and the fermenting wine of the ever new Kingdom. It's a tension between form and love, structure and Gospel, organisation and meaning. The symbols of the past threaten to become idolatrous. The old rituals assert themselves as absolute. The Spirit of the Jesus who violated Sabbath rules, avoided ritual purity, ate with sinners, and purged the temple, is Lord of our structures today – judging them, critiquing them, and guaranteeing that they are pliable skins for the new wine.

Addressing Poverty

CREST is a community development agency founded in 1971, in east London, out of a social responsibility committee set up by a local minister. It provides volunteers, and involves churches in their local communities. The local social services saw the local churches as fertile ground to recruit volunteers, and part of CREST's job was to co-ordinate these volunteers in their task of transformation.

By the 1990s, Alan Horne was at the helm, and CREST was facilitating a children's club in an Urban Priority Area, childrens' play schemes, a bereavement support scheme, a mental health befriending service, groups for older people with disabilities, and a pastoral worker concerned largely with the promotion of disability awareness in churches. No direct attempt is made to proselytise, though clients are aware that the help and support they receive come from Christian sources. Not all the volunteers are Christians. The children's club has paid sessional staff, but the befriending and bereavement services are entirely dependent upon volunteers. Alan explains:

The *bereavement* scheme aims to give the bereaved a safe and secure environment in which to express their feelings, for as long as they require. Volunteers are trained and supported by a professional supervisor. The volunteer contracts to meet with the bereaved person once a week for a session of between 15 and 60 minutes. Care is taken not to use the word 'counselling', because that is such a loaded word. We work with churches in different parts of the borough that have rooms suitable for these sessions.

The *befriending* service is primarily about matching up volunteers one-to-one with people in the community who have significant and enduring mental health problems. The volunteers contract to meet with the clients for around three hours per week. Within reason, the pair do whatever they want in that time! They may go out shopping, which for someone with a degree of agoraphobia can be a nightmare. Or they may elect to go for a meal, to the cinema or theatre, or perhaps for a day trip outside London. CREST has found very little problem in recruiting volunteers for this scheme; in 1997 it had around fifty. Alan Horne says:

I always hope that volunteers get an enormous amount of enjoyment out of what they do; if they're not learning from the work, and getting fed themselves, they can't provide for other people properly. On several occasions, volunteers have alerted us to the fact that clients have gone missing, and we have had to report the disappearance to the police! At the beginning, there were a lot of concerns about mental health, and the risk to female staff alone on the premises, but there have been no tricky incidents – people with mental health problems are far more likely to injure themselves than anyone else – and the project has certainly put us in a close and beneficial contact with the community. Churches are now, hopefully, more likely to be seen as warm centres of community in a cold and hostile urban environment.

A basic training course educates the volunteers on the essentials. Support of volunteers is crucial, because they are given a lot of responsibility. A paid staff member provides this, but, of course, there are difficulties in covering for the worker on leave and over bank holidays. Most of the time, the client simply needs someone to talk to, there is no deep counselling required. This is the kind of role which any committed Christian with a burden for people with mental health problems could perform. There would need to be a supporting infrastructure, but most local churches could provide this, along with the undergirding prayer support. 'Professionalism' should not be seen as a rude word, but it is also important that a project retains its transforming Christian base of core Gospel values.

Funding is not easy, but funding for secular social work is easier to get than money for explicit church work. Often, an organisation must be actively *providing a service* to the community in order to attract funding; there is little money available simply to *co-ordinate* the work of churches in this field. This creates a pressure to become more secularised. Of CREST's £150,000 annual budget, only £8,000 comes from specifically church sources, and Alan finds this to be a major issue. The Christian basis is central to the organisation, but it is also the most marginalised aspect. The solution, of course, is for Christians to be more generous in their giving towards such ministries, in order that the Christian values can remain in ascendance.

Getting 'Stuck In'

Anyone sensing a call to free people trapped by their poverty may be wondering how they can start. That is a theme that we will now begin to address in the remainder of this book.

For Bob Holman, a pioneering Christian community worker – though that title doesn't really do justice to the scope of his vision – the basic starting point is the belief that all people are created equal. On the outlying estates of Glasgow, *inequality* frequently rears its ugly head and laughs in the face of such values. Bob is passionately concerned about the devastating effect that poverty has upon people, sometimes pushing honest people into dubious practices as they struggle to survive.

The distribution of churches means that Christians are thin on the ground in Glasgow's hinterland, particularly in Easterhouse where he lives and works. There are few workers to help Bob in his task of helping the poor to break free from the shackles of poverty, and to escape from the meagre healthcare and lack of opportunity. Statistically, the women in Easterhouse die five years younger even than the women in nearby Glasgow. Poor healthcare, mediocre diet and damp all take their toll. The infant mortality rate is three times higher in Easterhouse than in more affluent areas. Bob says:

> It seems to me that, in the eyes of God, that is wrong. The children in care these days are predominantly the children of the poor. As a Christian, I believe that the Church should take a stand against such inequality. The Pro-Life campaigners put up candidates in the 1997 General Election, and I commend them for this, but I wish that these people were also Pro-Life in terms of saving children once they are born.

Acting Individually . . .

What can the church do strategically in its own neighbourhood? There are roles that the Church as a whole can perform, and tasks that are possible for individuals within it. The individual needs to ask: 'Where does God want me to be? Where does he want me to live? What level of income does he want me to have?' More Christians should give serious thought to moving into deprived areas, where they can be alongside people with great need.

This was what Jesus did; he didn't live in one of the great cities of his time, he dwelt in a small fishing community in the backwaters of the Roman empire. Had his mission simply been to proclaim a message of spiritual salvation, he would have done better to have had himself born to the wife of a Roman senator, and to have risen to become an Emperor, with absolute power to force his message across to the people. Instead, he chose a humble peasant girl for his mother, and a life amongst the deprived and the oppressed. Did he make a mistake? Or was his message far wider than the simple saving of souls? Surely his purpose was to teach a true and living way whereby people can be reconciled, not simply to God, but to their fellow men and women.

When Jesus came to earth, he wasn't a beggar, but he wasn't a rich man either; he seems to have lived at the lower end of sufficiency. Bob Holman deduced from this that Christians are called to live *modestly*, and to work towards the proper sharing of the resources that God has put on and in our planet.

'Global Christianity is wealthy,' says Sider in *Evangelism and Social Action*. 'Christians make up only one third (33%) of the world's population, but we receive about two-thirds (62%) of the world's total income each year. Tragically, we spend 97% of this on ourselves! One percent goes to secular charities. A mere 2% goes to all Christian work.'

... and Collectively

'We have to come, modestly, to live and work alongside Christians who have lived and worked here all their lives,' Bob says. It won't do to go to the poor with the aim of *teaching* them; it is first necessary to *learn* from them, then to *reflect* with them, before *participating* in the community, in *partnership* with them, to bring about lasting *transformation*.

Bob attends two churches in Easterhouse, a small Salvation Army congregation, and a larger Baptist church. The Sisters of Charity – the Roman Catholic order founded by Mother Teresa – have a small presence in the community, working alongside the other Christians. 'They have a nice balance between the spiritual and the social,' says Bob. The Church of Scotland has founded a community association, providing day care facilities, a youth club, a holiday project, and work with the elderly. The Salvation Army opened up a furniture store, selling second-hand furniture and appliances at reasonable prices. Bob himself joined with other residents to form FARE (Family Action in Rogerfield and Easterhouse).

When the caring people in the community began to realise that people had no ready source of financial loans – despite a 35,000 population, Easterhouse has no major bank – Christians stepped into the breach. People were taking legitimate loans from catalogue firms and bona fide credit agencies, but they were also finding themselves in the grip of loan sharks, charging them interest rates as high as *100 per cent per week!*

In his own book *FARE Dealing*, Bob describes how a young father called on him to tell him what he had already guessed, that the man had stolen Bob's wallet: 'By way of explanation, he showed me his knee, smashed in by a baseball bat. He too had borrowed to get things for his family and, on missing payments, had suffered the consequences. He stole from me to avoid another bashing.' On another occasion, an addict banged on Bob's door at two in the morning, demanding to borrow money for drugs. When Bob declined, the man brandished a savage-looking meat cleaver!

The Sisters of Charity called a public meeting and helped local people to form the North Easterhouse Credit Union. Local people saved money when they could and lent it to their needy neighbours at an interest rate not exceeding 12.6 per cent per year. By 1997, it had attracted 500 members. 'It's good for individuals, it's good for the community and, to my mind, it's Christian because it is helping families to survive,' Bob told us.

In Easterhouse, there is no major supermarket – only small local shops, which tend to be expensive, or vans which bring goods around, also at high prices. The Sisters of Charity helped the residents to set up a food co-operative. FARE's mini-bus would set off to the nearest large market and bring back good food at affordable rates. Bread was sold at 25p per loaf, whereas the local shops and the vans sold it at over 50p.

'I don't want to give the impression that this is just the social gospel, because, week in and week out, the churches are preaching the full Gospel,' Bob affirms. 'A lot of people come to the churches because their first contact with the Church is the fulfilment of a practical need.' Bob Holman has taken *eleven years* to forge the bonds of friendship that have made his work possible. With young people in particular, interest in Church tends to wane in their early teens, but Bob has found that – provided he can keep up a contact through greeting these young people in the street – some of them will begin to drift back into the Church in their early twenties. Many of the helpers at various youth clubs have 'come through' in this way. Bob has learned the importance of 'being there' for people.

When the local youngsters are faced with a choice between drifting into contact with the local criminal fraternity or attending youth clubs, it is vital that the youth clubs are made vibrant and attractive places. They are traditional clubs, offering the standard range of pool, table tennis and other typical youth activities, but they provide a valid alternative to the beginnings of a life of crime.

Here, in the simplest of church youth clubs, young people may learn more of the Christ who commanded that his followers were to go out into the world and be like salt in society. Salt is meant to be put on the meat to preserve it and to bring out the taste, and this is an excellent metaphor for the salvation and the lifestyle that comes from being obedient to Christ. Christians are meant to give life its savour. If a church doesn't go into its local community, but instead expects people to come to them, this is the equivalent of taking a piece of meat and totally engulfing it in salt. Such meat then becomes too salty to eat, and it is no use for anything. The Christians in Easterhouse are ready to step out into the community, and to deposit themselves sacrificially into the red raw meat of people's lives.

Salt of the Earth . . .

Housing in Easterhouse has thankfully improved in recent years, but drug abuse has worsened. Bob considers that drug abuse will never be adequately tackled until the problem of unemployment is tackled. Young people take drugs because their life has no meaning, and they are bored out of their skulls. Traditionally, local people gained status through holding down physically-demanding manual jobs, often underground in the coal mines that have now closed.

Now, you become a 'hard man' in the community by sticking a needle in your arm and filling your veins with heroin . . .

In response to those needs, FARE now employs a former rock musician, to develop music skills amongst young people who are on the verge of embracing the drug culture, and who think playing table tennis in a youth club is a bit too 'sissy'. He gives guitar lessons, and takes the young people on visits to recording studios. It's exciting, but legitimate – and a lot safer than 'shooting up' drugs.

Counselling people who are drug abusers is a specialised ministry; Bob would like to see trained and experienced Christians moving into the area to take on the work, offering friendship and practical help. As it is, the Christians in Easterhouse have had to forge strong partnerships with secular relief agencies. Such partnerships are important in the war against poverty, as local Christians struggle to be salt and light in their communities.

. . . Light of the World

'There is always a danger that I will become "The Charity Man", giving to people all the time,' Bob admits.

This can upset people. Relationships need to be *reciprocal*, so the other party has the opportunity to give back now and again, and to participate in the work that is being done with them. Local people *own* the project because only the local people can attend the AGM and be voted on to the FARE committee. This willingness to have people participate has helped to build good relationships with schools, which allow the youth clubs to be run on their premises.

One of the consequences of poverty is never being able to afford a holiday. Bob has helped to address this disadvantage by helping to pioneer a holiday scheme for children. The scheme has purchased a twelve-bed caravan which is let out at £100 per week to provide a cheap holiday for local families who otherwise would not be able to afford to go away anywhere. It is now run entirely by two of FARE's committee members, so local people are providing holiday opportunities for other local people, in a classic example of good community development practice.

So how can a community-run project like FARE be described as 'Christian'? Bob Holman explains:

> Social workers have told us that, without the work of FARE, a lot more local children would have been taken into care. I think *that* is Christian. I don't think God wants families to break up! If we manage to stop a couple of kids from going down the drug route, *that* is Christian, because it is building the kind of society that God wants. The icing on the cake is when some of these people *do* become Christians. But we never get into the position of saying, 'You can't come to youth club unless you come to church.'

Regarding training, Bob Holman believes in throwing people in the deep end as a volunteer. 'One of the local dads proved himself very adept as a volunteer in one of the local youth clubs, so we have now taken him on as a full-time worker. Hopefully, he will one day get himself a qualification but, for the moment, he is learning on the job.'

Bob tells of a local man who committed suicide, and of the devastating effect this had on the man's wife and children. Bob has come to know the family over several years, largely through the local youth club. On one occasion the widow was arrested by the police early one morning, and immediately turned to Bob for appropriate help. The eldest son is a heroin addict, and Bob is working with the youngest – who has already been expelled from two schools – with the simple aim of keeping him away from crime and drugs.

This particular family was very inhibited as a result of its traumatic history, but the woman one day produced a sheaf of papers on which she had written about herself. Bob was able to arrange for one of these articles to be published. The woman received payment for this, but publication helped to raise her self-confidence and esteem, through contributing something in return for the help she received. Further publications followed, and the woman's articulation is helping to make others aware of the problems within the area, and of the good work that is shining a light into the dark corners of Easterhouse. For Bob, it makes all the hard work seem worthwhile.

Questions

- What other reasons can you think of to avoid helping in the war on poverty?
- What do you think it feels like to be poor, and then to escape from that poverty?
- What would you have done if you had been in Bob Holman's position, threatened with a meat cleaver on your own doorstep?
- In what other ways could Christians help the people of Easterhouse?
- What have you learned through studying Bob's situation (and the two types of church which David Evans described) that you could apply in your own situation?

6

Cry Justice!

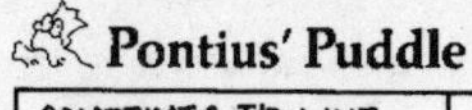

It is, perhaps, the ultimate nightmare.

On a very ordinary day, you walk through the village where you have walked countless times before. Perhaps you are shopping, walking your dog, or visiting a friend. This day is different, however. Today, you are stopped short by a searing pain, a flash and a deafening explosion.

You awake in a seedy hospital, swathed in bandages. But the pain you feel in your legs is purely imaginary, *because your legs are not there any more . . .*

You have trodden on a landmine, which shattered your life into as many little pieces as your broken body. Yet your tragedy will go unreported in any newspaper, and this atrocity will not make the evening news bulletin, because this is Cambodia. Here, you are just another statistic.

Where's the Justice?

The figures make grim reading. Cambodia has 35,000 amputees – innocent casualties of a cruel weapon of war that makes killing so simple and anonymous. Militarily, it is better to maim your enemy than to kill him. That way, vital medical resources will be employed to treat and evacuate the wounded, whose injuries will have a detrimental psychological effect on morale. But a landmine cannot choose between you or a soldier. A mine does not know when the war is over.

Coming through nine years of Cambodia's civil war unscathed, Romdol was gathering bamboo shoots in the jungle one day when she heard the quiet 'click' of a detonator underfoot. With a roar, she was flung through the air, her left leg shattered. Her friend came to help her, there was another 'click', and the two maimed girls were found together, after five hours in terrible pain. Their potential for work, marriage and children – their hope for full acceptance in community life – has been cut short.

Blameless casualties often survive the immediate blast, only to die from blood loss or infection. The blast of a landmine – some of them look more like toys than weapons – can drive dirt, bone fragments and shrapnel deep into the injury. The cost of treatment, where treatment is available, stretches resources to breaking point and contributes to the impoverishment of whole villages. The rural communities of Cambodia are characterised by chronic health problems, an inadequate water supply and a fragile food production system. At times the world looks so grim, it can seem as though the four horsemen are practising for the Apocalypse.

In 1995 there were an estimated 100 million anti-personnel mines lying scattered like military confetti around the world, with a similar number in government stockpiles – enough to maim 4 per cent of the global population. Mines have claimed more than a million innocent targets in the past twenty-five years. Today and every day, an average of *seventy* people will be killed or injured by a landmine – mainly civilians, in peacetime. A simple plastic mine, undetectable once buried, costs about £2 to manufacture; but the rehabilitation of its prey costs 1,000 times more.

Hope on the Killing Fields

What are Christians doing about this terrible curse?

Christian relief agency World Vision is actively involved in campaigning, medical care, and the clearing of mine fields. Jaisankar Sarma, who heads World Vision Cambodia, explains that a horrific *one in every 236* Cambodians is a landmine victim. 'This is not what God intended for Cambodia! When God said "good" when he created the world, he included Cambodia and its people as well.'

Jaisankar is not Cambodian-born himself. He comes from a middle-class Hindu family, from the top Brahmin caste, and was raised close to Madras. He became a Christian in 1982 while studying at an agricultural college – when he heard an Indian evangelist preaching from Psalm 51:10 – but he soon found himself financially rejected by his family. Searching for the route God wanted his life to take, he accepted a short-term placement with a Christian organisation, though his own preference was to work for a secular company where he could be a witness for Christ. However, he was disappointed by the low standards he found in that organisation, and he left to take a posting with World Vision only as a stop-gap arrangement – but God had other ideas.

'Twelve years later, I'm still here! The God I worship has a bias for the poor, and that understanding helped me to work with the poor in a way that reflects God's character and activity.' He started in a mundane staff training job and ended up, accidentally, as National Director in Cambodia – where his skills as an agriculturist have been invaluable in restoring minefields into useable agricultural land.

World Vision works in some of the most heavily mined areas of Cambodia, working with communities to build up their ability to cope economically, while giving guidance on ways to avoid becoming victims. We also help hospitals to cope better with treating the injuries of landmine victims, and run projects to train the maimed in the skills that will restore their self-confidence and make them useful members of the community once more.

Apocalypse Riders' Steeplechase?

'You cannot easily change the damage caused by the war, or caused by the systematic breaking of relationships, or the loss of dignity,' says Meas Nee, a Khmer. 'You cannot easily change the damage done by the meetings held in fear, or the meetings at which the people were harangued by propaganda. The mind is paralysed by such things so the way forward is slowly, carefully.'

The cruel injustice heaped upon the endangered population by the minefields gives new dimensions to the already horrendous poverty of the area, affirms Ian Wallace, Tear Fund's International Services Group Director:

In Cambodia, poverty is not simply physical. As a result of the traumatic physical history, it is also a mental and spiritual one, where people have been subject to genocide. People have seen the future as a continuation of the past, and to present a bright hopeful future is challenging. Relief agencies there have focused on allowing people to make choices, and to make mistakes within those choices, but not to be judgmental towards themselves. They are, instead, encouraged to reflect.

Many Cambodian villages possess but a single open well to provide water for all the villagers' needs. On one occasion, a development agency worked with a particular village to dig a much-needed new well. Villages are often willing to offer a few of their men to construct a well, so long as an outside organisation pays for the materials; but reaction to change, religious superstition and past politics (the Khmer Rouge routinely killed potential activists) makes them passive towards transformation. This time, a local committee was assembled and given the power to oversee this, while the development agency took a hands-off approach. What happened? Months passed and there was no well and no money! Someone ran off with the funding that had been provided.

The development agency used this event to bring the villagers into reflection on what had happened; because they didn't sit in judgment on the villagers who had allowed this to happen, the villagers didn't judge themselves. They simply asked the villagers what they had *learned* from this disaster, and to work out for themselves what they could do to prevent the same thing from happening again. It sounds 'soft', but the approach produced more lasting results than if the well had been dug as originally planned. Further funding could be supplied to dig the well, but no amount of money could have bought the change of attitude and perception that came from hard-fought reflection in their struggle to achieve a viable future.

What do we in the so-called developed world learn from this? That in the struggle for social justice, there's no need to make a drama out of a crisis! Recriminations are debilitating and counter-productive, but something good can be rescued from a catastrophe if the participants come to understand enough to prevent the same occurrence from repeating itself. It is necessary to be realistic about the process, involving the appropriate people and encouraging trust and respect amongst all involved.

Advocate for the Poor

Many disadvantaged people are not merely poor people in need of freedom from poverty, they are also the victims of injustice and oppression. They are in need of *empowerment* if they are ever to be truly free from poverty.

Clive Furness is a qualified barrister, who practises for free as an advocate working with powerless people who have suffered from mental health problems. He supports and/or represents them, with social services officials, but also anywhere that disabled people might have difficulties. In the mental health arena, for example, the training of psychiatrists does not always lead to good continuity of patient care.

Clive found himself particularly useful to guileless people trying to communicate with consultants:

Patients are enormously vulnerable and lack power. Consultants have an enormous amount of power. In one hospital, locum consultants who had not got to know their patients appeared to carry the attitude that they were the ones who knew best. I worked with patients prior to a ward round, helping them to work out what they wanted to say, and how they were going to say it.

Success is very difficult to measure. In terms of making sure that patients' views were heard, I had quite a high degree of success, but that doesn't always mean that the outcome was the one that the patient desired. Sometimes consultants gave good answers to the questions that we had, which satisfied the patient. On other occasions, we influenced the course of treatment, putting forward a different course of treatment that was at least as valid; and sometimes we just felt that we were beating our heads against a brick wall – particularly with those patients who had been sectioned. We managed to institute a number of management reviews, though I didn't do tribunals, because there was legal aid available.

It is *not* necessary to have any legal expertise in order to be an advocate. This is a role which any lay Christian could take on, given adequate preparation and support. Clive maintains:

Personally I don't think legal training is essential; what is necessary is the ability to get on with people who are sometimes quite upset. Their behaviour can be very strange at times, and they make demands that are not always appropriate. You have to work with them patiently and clearly, to formulate demands that are realistic given the situation in which they find themselves.

Secondly, you help them to put those demands and desires across to professionals. A lawyer's training is very good for this, but it is not vital. Some of the best advocates are family members. I would approach the problems from an intellectual level, putting things in order and in a neat framework and presenting them in an ordered fashion; but a mother or brother might not go about it in the same way – they might use more emotional force than I would myself, but they get similar results.

Here is an area where ordinary Christians can make a substantial difference in their communities. Church sponsored projects need to train and empower ordinary Christians instead of bringing in expensive professionals. They should work on a human scale, beginning with small groups to encourage individual contributions, before any thought is given to larger-scale work.

In helping poor people to express themselves clearly to authority figures with whom they may be in conflict, an advocate is 'doing justice' by helping to bring about agreement and reconciliation between warring parties. But there are three other forms of justice that are needed by the oppressed. *First*, there is the need for political change that will redress the unjust imbalance in ownership of resources, which we can help to bring about by campaigning and by lobbying politicians. *Second*, there is a need for honesty in our personal dealings, ensuring that the workers who produce the goods we buy are not exploited – that the 'bargain' we bought yesterday is justified, and wasn't made possible through unjust employment conditions (we will consider these two types of justice in chapters 8–10). *Third*, there is the need for groups or networks of believers *who demonstrate justice through their concerns, lifestyle and activities.* Here's an example of the latter.

The Shelter of our Lives

Clive Furness is also a co-founder of Newham Nightshelter, which started in the winter of 1992–3. At an evangelistic rally in the early seventies, Clive had felt a very strong call to work with the homeless; the call was met after a couple of decades of experience in youth and community work. While he was working near London's Lincoln's Inn Fields – at the time being closed down as a primary sleeping place for many powerless homeless people – seeing a homeless person on the streets brought the old feelings back with a vengeance:

> I counted eighty-four people sleeping in shop doorways, within a very small physical space. My first instinct was to do something through my local church, in Plaistow. Our building was available but we lacked the people to staff a shelter. Shortly afterwards I received a letter from the local Christian-run Community Renewal Programme, calling a meeting to explore ways in which churches could work together. Twenty people came to the first meeting, and eighty to the second. Six churches and one community centre committed themselves to help, and the local Housing Department gave its backing.

A temporary Nightshelter was set up to run for four weeks in January 1993, operating from different premises each night of the week. It went so well, that the scheme was extended for a further six weeks. Several churches working together in partnership had managed to achieve something that had proved impossible for Clive's church on its own! Though no more than eleven homeless people slept over at any one time, the feedback from local Christians was so positive that a decision was taken to run the scheme again the following year. The believers had been able, not just to offer physical shelter and food, but to share with these poor powerless people the shelter of their own Christian lives, radiant and appealing to those who had lost their serenity in the storm of life.

Gimme Shelter!

Clive says of the project:

> Individual Christians have been involved, not simply because they wanted to do something for the Nightshelter, but *because the work has been part of the mission with which their particular church has felt called to be involved.* The people in the churches have felt a very strong ownership of the project. All major denominations have been involved in the delivery of the product over the past few years. Catholics through to African Pentecostalists are involved in running it. The Bishop of Barking, Roger Sainsbury, remarked that it has been the best example of churches working together that he has seen in his seven years as bishop.
>
> I can't think of any problems that cropped up over different styles of churchmanship. The general reaction has been that it is very good to work with other Christians! There has been no need for any *denial*; we haven't asked people to give up any part of their own Christian heritage, and people of different theological backgrounds have found it easy to respect the views of those from very different church traditions. Everybody felt that it was part of their own ministry, both as individual Christians, and as part of the church body.

Though each church provides many of the volunteers for the one weeknight that the shelter operates from its own premises, other volunteers join them from neighbouring churches that don't have a night of their own. As the Nightshelter moves from church to church, its atmosphere and style changes perceptibly from night to night, as each night develops its own ethos. An annual conference acts as a vehicle for new ideas, and paid staff have been brought in to help support the volunteers.

Many local charities have fought shy of employing paid staff, often for fear that the staff may 'take over' the project. *It is vital that any staff recruited are made keenly aware that they are there to serve the volunteers, and not vice versa.* Ownership must always remain in the hands of the volunteers. Both the Nightshelter and another Christian-run resettlement scheme operating in Newham have experienced problems with their staff. It's human nature for people to resent intrusion on to their 'private territory', and many projects find that tensions exist between staff and trustees, over the demarcation of responsibilities. Clive says:

> The unpaid volunteers feel that they have done the work, and that they *are* experts at it. The staff feel that they are being paid to *become* experts at it, and that creates problems. There are very different ways in which people work. The staff are being asked to work with very different groups of people each day, creating problems that need to be managed – but these are not insurmountable. Discipline is one area of difficulty; sometimes a volunteer will end up exacerbating a problem with a particular client, that the staff are trying to calm. Sometimes staff will innocently usurp the role of the volunteers. With the Nightshelter, authority is passed from a volunteer shift-leader to a member of staff at some point during the night, and this can create a conflict as the volunteers feel they are losing responsibility, though they are also gaining a safety element simply through having a member of staff present throughout the night.
>
> I deal with these problems mainly by talking to the staff. An extensive training programme is carried out with the volunteers prior to opening each winter, but the only people *ultimately* that I can control are the staff. I put up with occasionally eccentric behaviour on the part of volunteers, because they are going to be there year after year, while the staff are only on short-term contracts. It is their job to make the work safer for the volunteers, and to assist in making the work happen, through support and facilitation. Each shelter has one or two people who represent them on a co-ordinating committee that meets monthly, as a forum to discuss policy and problems – though this is very much an arm's-length management of the situation.

It's important to get to know all the volunteers, and to develop a personal relationship with as many as possible.

People Power

Clive would like to see much greater support for homeless people in terms of offering choice in housing, as he struggles to move his hapless clients from a dependency frame to a situation where they can contribute. Hostels are getting a better name, though the larger ones still tend to lack any sense of community; powerless people feel very anonymous within them. The unpretentious homeless generally sleep in their day clothes, for fear of having them stolen if they take them off; when you own very little, the risk of losing everything is infinitely greater.

The Nightshelter's volunteer-to-client ratio used to be 1:2, but it has now grown to 1:5 as the number of users has increased dramatically. These crushed people are emotionally bruised and in need of time and support, from the networks of Christians who – in operating the Nightshelter – are demonstrating God's justice for the poor and oppressed.

It's difficult to empower the clients to have a say in the running of the project, because it is not the oppressed users and ex-users who are going to make the scheme work – it's the faithful Christians who contribute the bulk of the time and money. The lay Christians must be empowered to run the project, but Christians, other helpers, and clients alike are deserving of empowerment to combat oppression and lack of choices in their own lives.

The scheme started with a negligible financial input, with bedding in the form of a dozen judo mats being moved from shelter to shelter each night. Once it had established a track record, funding – £70,000 for 1997 – became easier. Anyone seeking to emulate the work elsewhere needs to start by empowering churches and individual Christians to demonstrate God's justice, starting *where they are at now!*

Let willing volunteers come in and do whatever they can for the time they have available, and that is a good beginning. There will be times, though, when it all seems to get too much. There never seem to be enough people available, or enough hours free from the people you've got. The work can seem insignificant compared with the problems to be overcome. At these discouraging moments when the road ahead seems interminable, it is important to remember that the longest journey begins with a single step. When each stride is made prayerfully, with Jesus alongside, the way seems easier because we are joining in *The Mustard Seed Conspiracy*. In his book of that title, Tom Sine explains how it is time to teach the planet to sing and dance:

> It is still God's policy to work through the embarrassingly insignificant to change the world and create his future. He wants to use your life and mine to make a difference in his world. Just as Jesus invited that first unlikely bunch of fishermen, so he invites us to abandon our boats and our nets, and join him in the adventure of changing the world.

Faith in Action

People join the adventure in many different ways. Many are drawn into new and innovative schemes from disillusionment with old ways, and an often ill-defined awareness that 'there must be a better way than this . . .' The blunt feeling of dissatisfaction turns up first, like a nagging toothache, and then the precise articulation arrives later. David Ainge is an Anglican priest who has been associated with one particular pioneering work since 1987:

> In my previous parish in Dagenham, we had a jumble sale. At the end, there were still twenty-three bags of jumble left over! The ragman came and gave us three pounds for the lot. We were fuming with rage at the injustice. We knew that much of the clothing was good stuff. A month or so later, I visited a friend who put me in touch with Faith in Action . . .

Faith in Action is a charity that forges church-to-church links between UK churches and congregations in East Africa. It makes practical provision of shoes, clothing, bedding, suits for ministers, and other items that are readily discarded in the West, but when repaired and properly presented are acceptable to powerless and destitute people in the Third World. Their dignity is restored by the receiving, as the clothing begins to empower them by restoring their self-worth. Good quality clothing, often from jumble sales, but also specifically donated by Christians up and down the UK, is lovingly washed and repaired as necessary. The restored clothing is then packed in old apple boxes. Each individual apple box may contain anything from three or four blankets to twenty or so items of children's clothing.

Prior to transit, these boxes are stored in one of six twenty-foot containers, housed in lock-up garages and church car parks all over Britain. When each container is full, its store of cloth-filled apple boxes is transferred into a sturdier container, rented from P&O, who then organise the sea transport overseas. Each container holds 600 apple boxes, and eighteen containers have been sent to Malawi alone over the ten years up to 1997. In that time, less than half a container load has been subject to pilfering, so hundreds of thousands of items have been received by the pastors in Malawi, freely distributed to outlying villages, and gratefully received. 'This has been a practical, hands-on operation enabling people who have little cash to make a massive investment. As soon as I announce in church that we've run out of clothing to send, that's the cue for the front doorbell to ring with bin bags full of good quality used clothing.'

Fashionable Giving

Some of us walk around in worn clothing, believing that money for a new shirt or jacket could better be spent on the Lord's work elsewhere. Other Christians overdress to the point of vanity, spending hundreds of pounds per month on new clothing. But by passing on our clothing while it is still in good condition, it's easier to justify reasonable personal expenditure on replacements for our wardrobe to maintain our own professional appearance. David Ainge says:

> We've been involved in house clearances when someone has died, as well as clearances when someone has changed their wardrobe. But we have also attracted the attention of large clothing manufacturers, who have needed somewhere responsible to offload surplus garments that are now out of fashion.
>
> Recently, a prison in Suffolk has changed from being a men's prison to being a women's prison. Clearly the clothing that was suitable for male inmates is no longer viable for the women. The discarded items would have had to be incinerated, until one of our packing groups close to the prison let it be known that they would welcome any surplus items. They guaranteed to send these surplus items outside the EEC for free distribution. Hundreds of pairs of trousers were received, in excellent condition. We had a similar experience when British Caledonian Airways were bought up by British Airways. Thousands of unwanted aircraft blankets with the former logo were given to us, just at the time the problems were beginning in Albania. We sent half the blankets to Albania, and the other half to Africa.

Soap, towels, garden tools and other household items that we take for granted in the West are often in short supply in the developing world. Sub-standard toothbrushes were donated by a well-known manufacturer, and these are now helping to save teeth in Malawi. The British consumer market is very fussy over what it will accept, and the slightest defect consigns goods to the scrap bin. Abroad, the needy are less choosy, and they welcome items whose colouring or style would be rejected by pernickety British shoppers. However, it is necessary to send only clothing that is culturally acceptable to the Africans. With a little initiative – and the goodwill of secular manufacturers – Christians in partnership can actually exploit the fickleness of consumer society for the advantage of the Third World's poorer citizens!

Local Trading Standards departments confiscate pirated designer goods and, once the relevant court cases have been completed, by law the counterfeit goods have to be incinerated or *disposed of outside the EEC*; enter Faith in Action, and the African poor in dire need of clothing. There are people in southern Malawi who are now walking around in counterfeit Nike track suits!

'All of Faith in Action's work is done on a voluntary basis,' says David. No one gets paid.

The nearest thing we have to office premises is the home of Martin and Sally Jeffrey, the couple who started the charity, in Crawley. The main overhead is transport cost – it takes around £7 to get each apple box to Malawi, door-to-door. God is great, it's a miracle the way the money comes in. We've never appealed for money, but lots of individuals give lots of small amounts. It's very encouraging. Everyone gives of their time, talents and money – and they are *empowered* through feeling that their work is valued by those less fortunate than themselves. We receive regular reports back, and Sally flies to Malawi several times per year, at her own expense. She's often been the only white person in the village, from one year to the next.

We have tried to ensure that the African church doesn't become over-dependent upon white middle-class Britons. There are lots of things we would like to have done, but for which we have not had the money. It's fair to say that the Africans have not understood our hesitance, because in African society the white people live in enormous houses and can afford anything.

The Great Unwashed

Everything gets washed before it is sent – there are horror stories of other charities who have sent unwashed clothing, only for a consignment to arrive six months later in a rancid condition, stinking to high heaven. Each item is bagged separately in a clear polythene bag, sealed and labelled in the national language, with the words

'This comes to you in the name of the Lord Jesus.' As well as being a corporate demonstration of the Church's concern for justice, *this is also very effective outreach*. The pastors in Malawi have described the operation as a major evangelistic tool for them. The local people begin to reflect on *why* they have become the recipients of such help. They begin to reason: 'If these Christians in Britain, whom we have never met, love us that much, then the God they worship and serve must be a wonderful God,' and they begin to respond in simple faith and trust.

'We've found that, when you put your faith into action, not only is the action appreciated, but so too is the faith,' says David. Not only are others touched by the kindness of Christians, the believers often find that their *own* faith develops and is deepened. David has seen enormous transformation in the two British churches he has pastored where the Faith in Action programme has been followed.

In the first church, mission activity was a marginal activity; the congregation thought they were too poor to financially support overseas mission. They took a familiar view: 'We don't understand development issues, and even if we did, we have enough problems of our own.' Though the second church has a long history of supporting overseas mission, it too found that the opportunity to become 'hands-on' and to participate in a practical initiative empowered its members and substantially enriched its communal life. By becoming partners in the fight to bring equality and social justice to the poor and oppressed, they received a startling insight into the life and work of Christians abroad – not only Anglicans, since the churches in Malawi are independent Pentecostals.

They discovered that, as parts of the body of Christ, we may be in different camps but we are at least on the same encampment. Working together, meeting common needs, and enabling others to work with our resources, has developed a wonderful partnership. When the Malawi ministers have visited Britain to meet the packing groups, the joy and delight actually to put a face to a name has been terrific. It's easy to preach about the worldwide Christian community, but it is so much better to actually meet members of that community, face-to-face, in your own home. It's been an eye-opener to the whole body of Christ.

Questions and Exercises

- How do *you* think those in church leadership could increase the competence and expertise of the church to carry out its work?
- In church staff recruitment, what do *you* think should be the key elements of job description with regard to volunteer input?
- How does your church empower its members?
- How is a 'releasing' mentality, in leadership, preferable to a 'controlling' mentality, in relation to work undertaken by church members?
- Can you think of a project that a church, or a committed group of individuals, could initiate that would tackle the justice issues present in your community?

7

Cry Mercy!

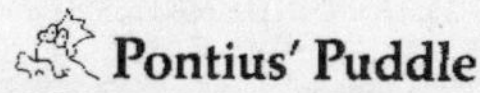

Noddy and Big Ears were driving through Toytown one day, alongside their overseas friend with the 'not politically correct' name. The local community policeman threatened to 'nick' Noddy for insulting behaviour – for calling him 'Plod' instead of 'Bill'. Then a social worker told Noddy that he was being deeply abhorrent to disabled people by calling his friend with the large lobes such a vile name.

After that, Noddy and his two friends were stopped by a young woman who asked them if they wanted to do 'business'. Noddy couldn't think what she meant. Then a youth with his baseball cap on backwards enquired whether the threesome could 'use some blow'. Some other young people enquired where 'Charley Horse' could be found. Another man invited Noddy and his friends to a 'cottage', but this turned out to be a public lavatory! Then the man offered money and asked Noddy how long he had been 'a rent boy'. The three friends went home feeling very confused.

'This would never have happened in Enid Blyton's day,' said Noddy.

'Whatever has happened to our childhood?' sighed his two friends.

In the modern world, children grow up too quickly, and the naivety of stories that would have enchanted an earlier generation is ridiculed and denounced by sophisticates who insist on taking the worst possible view of simple diversions. Other children lose their innocence very quickly, as adults try to exploit their youthfulness. Not allowing children to be children, makes them adults too quickly.

Pastor David Connolly discovers this anew each day on the streets of Wavertree, Liverpool. On one occasion, he discovered that a group of children from his church club had purchased some ecstasy tablets from a local dealer. David took the tablets and demanded to know the name and address of the dealer, and how much had been paid for them. He stormed over to the dealer's house and hammered on the door, ignoring the threats of violence that came from inside. When the dealer came to the door, David demanded that he return the children's money: 'And don't you go selling drugs to our kids any more!' Perhaps through surprise and shock that anyone would dare to challenge his right to corrupt young lives, the dealer returned the money. Pointedly, David did not return the ecstasy tablets, but took them off for disposal!

David's church – aptly named Frontline – has established a creche for young mothers. Many of the mothers who use the facility are scarcely out of childhood themselves. The values of the permissive society have made them old before their time. Now this dynamic church has launched *Kidz Club*, 'a fast and furious hour of fun' on a Saturday morning. From it has grown a visitation programme intended to build relationships from the church into the children's families. It offers a solid alternative to the kind of lifestyle that produces fourteen-year-old mothers who are 'on the game' to feed their addiction to crack cocaine . . .

On the Frontline

Other development projects run by Frontline include *Streetwise*, an outreach into the community. It works particularly with the homeless and marginalised through a soup kitchen van, operating for three evenings per week. An NHS nurse is on hand once a week to assist in a medical capacity. The elderly and housebound are also helped by this service, in conjunction with a luncheon club, with assistance from Age Concern. A community team and a drop-in centre round off this aspect of the work. 'The idea is to build relationships,' David affirms.

Many of these projects operate from the Frontline Centre, a former Army drillhall, set in an area dominated by prevailing despair and an impression of hopelessness. There is a keen sense of urgency to redress the deteriorating conditions and fabric of the neighbourhood, which is hallmarked by poverty, family breakdown, drug abuse, and mental health difficulties. Frontline's prime focus is *investment in the individuals that make up this community.*

Each activity stems from the results of detailed research, analysis of needs, current provision, and consultation with other organisations. Most of the volunteers – some of whom work full-time without pay – live within the community and witness the problems at first hand. With many activities, the users are encouraged to participate in the running, as Frontline struggles to empower its community. It is important that people are willing to take on responsibility, and to bear the pain of an open-ended commitment.

'We want the church to feel like home to its members. Just because a church grows to a large size should not stop it being a home. As long as individuals can keep a strong affinity to the values and vision of the church, can find their place of function and be bonded in through a circle of close-knit relationships, then it will still feel like home,' says David.

'The heart of a community is the values that keep it together. Transformation of a community is therefore the transformation of its values,' echoes C. B. Samuel, General Director of EFICOR, an organisation working in rural India, whose training is geared to shape, guide and build transformed lives. 'We believe that such an effort is a process and not a performance. *It is the process of translating one's inner experience of Christ into actions of hope for the poor and the marginalised.*'

Bridge Building

When Terry Jones arrived as pastor of Liverpool's Toxteth Tabernacle, in 1989, there was little money to pay his salary; nowhere for him to live; and only twenty-five members. Terry took a deep breath and got on with the job, feeling passionately that this was the place to which God had called him. Like Nehemiah, he arrived with a vision to restore a broken city:

> So many of the principles in that Bible book seemed to apply both to Liverpool and to the local church situation in which I found myself. For the first year, I said nothing to anyone about my plans and intentions; to do so could easily have been seen as patronising. Instead I began to network, going out wherever I could simply to learn my way around. Shops, clubs, doctors' surgeries, educational welfare offices, pubs and schools all received a visit. I found out what people did, and what they considered to be the needs of the area.

Out of those visits – and through prayer and consultation – a vision began to dawn for the work that needed to be done. In an educational welfare office, Terry heard the story about a troublesome pupil who decided that he wanted to make for himself, of all things, a suit of armour out of cardboard! The officer provided the materials and, within weeks, the young lad had fashioned for himself an immaculate suit of cardboard armour. Clearly here was a very capable person who needed only someone to believe in his abilities and to nurture them. Terry began to wonder how many other young people were creatively frustrated by the demands of the daily struggle for survival in urban Liverpool. Amongst the needs and stresses of inner-city life, local people owned latent skills and unfulfilled dreams to which the church could begin to make a response.

Surveys often play a significant role in enabling a church to uncover the hidden needs of the community around it, and this was certainly true for the Toxteth 'Tab'. A mums-and-toddlers club was going nowhere, because the mums didn't need somewhere simply to meet other mums – they actually wanted somewhere they could *leave* their children to go off and attend to other matters. The church's survey showed an overwhelming need for a playgroup, catering for two- to four-year-olds.

We made this our first step in building a bridge into the community. Though it had been a major preaching centre attracting big-name outside speakers, our church had only one couple left who actually lived in Toxteth – this notorious Liverpool 8 area where serious rioting had taken place only a few years earlier. The rest of the congregation commuted in from the suburbs. Unlike Frontline, we had lost all sense of serving a community in a relevant way; indeed the community had castigated us for our inability to identify with the needs of the area.

Step by Step

By this time, Terry and his family had found somewhere to live, and because of God's provision he had not gone without anything he needed, despite a small congregation unable to pay its pastor anything like a living wage. Two UK Baptist churches rallied around to help support Terry financially, and through sending teams to help with the work. His car had been smashed, bikes stolen, and stones thrown at his windows, but Terry considered this to be 'par for the course' and got on with his job.

Even while struggling to put right years of neglect, the Tabernacle began to initiate projects to address the perceived needs of the people of the area. Through reflection, and in partnership with distant suburban churches sharing from their prosperity, the process of transformation began. Ten thousand pounds were raised to equip a playgroup on the church premises, with two full-time paid staff and several volunteer helpers: 'Our philosophy was to see how *much* we could pay people, not how little. We always seek to pay people the top rate, to give them worth, dignity and self-esteem. God has always honoured that.'

Twenty-five children attend the playgroup, with a waiting list of many parents who would like their children to attend. One of the leaders took a secular NVQ childcare course for a year, rewrote the course material to reflect a Christian ethos, and had her revisions accepted by the secular authorities. Church members visit the children's families at home, giving the congregation contacts deeper into the community.

The regeneration of the local community continued apace, in 1993, with a coffee shop initiative – more like a quality restaurant – where a friendly atmosphere and good food have made the church's former lounge into an oasis of peace for a troubled neighbourhood. Local employment has been facilitated through mothers being able to leave their children in safe care and take on part-time jobs; posts have been created within the playgroup itself; and the coffee shop that has stemmed from the work has given some of the catering staff their first-ever wage packets. Terry learned – like Nehemiah – that though it was right to keep his sights aimed high and to have large-scale plans for the future, those plans could only be brought to fruition by building a little bit at a time.

The excitement builds once you've achieved something that you originally thought was beyond your capabilities. Some of our staff felt that they were worthless, but their success gave them such a sense of dignity and self-esteem that they could take a further step. I 'modelled faith' to them by coming here before there was finance available to pay my salary, and every one of our current thirteen staff has also come before there was money available to pay them. The congregation has been gratefully encouraged by the way God has provided.

Four years on, the coffee shop was well recognised in the under-privileged local community, and the local people no longer have any reservations about coming on to church property. Though coffee shops often attract a largely female clientele, Terry has known times when it has been packed with local men, all being gently touched by the peaceful atmosphere. Street gangs and local 'hard men' have been through the portals, without incident.

'The coffee shop is more "church" than our Sunday services,' Terry has come to feel. 'We have laughter, social relationships, a sense of communion and a shared interest in each other's lives. Everything that you would want a good church to do, and be, is being expressed in the coffee shop.'

The number of burglaries and instances of smashed windows has fallen drastically, as local people have come to 'own' the church and its work for themselves. After a bag was stolen, a local man approached the people he believed to be responsible and told them firmly: 'Don't you be stealing anything from the Tab any more! Some of us believe in what they are doing!' *Here was a non-Christian prepared to defend the Christian ministry taking place in his neighbourhood.*

Effective Evangelism

Next, the 3,000 sq. ft basement was gutted and renovated, to turn it into a training centre. There are pottery, woodwork and textile sections and an IT area in this new skills school catering for fourteen- to sixteen-year-olds who have been excluded from conventional education. Vocational, practical and life skills are taught, and efforts are made to put the young people into work placements once they turn sixteen. Most of the staff are Christians, and those who are not are clearly influenced by their Christian colleagues in many subtle ways, as reflection takes place alongside the busy schedule of activity. The three projects running by 1997 all fed into one another to produce a unified outreach into the local neighbourhood, and several other projects were in the planning stage, including medical facilities. This social action has led organically into direct evangelism, in the form of three major missions, as Terry explains:

> We weren't looking to reap, but simply to make ourselves visually known on the streets. For three years running we ran a mission that we called *First Steps*. The initial year, we were joined by sixty outsiders from YWAM augmenting just *three* local people; the second year, *nine* indigenous people joined the thirty-person outside team; and on the third occasion *twenty-nine* local people outnumbered the fifteen outsiders. It was thrilling!

The local Christians had benefited by on-the-job training, learning from the experienced missioners by working alongside them and reflecting on the activities they saw take place.

As time went by, the local Christians wanted to *own* the work; it soon changed from something that outsiders were doing in partnership with them, to an activity they could perform for themselves, once their confidence had grown. The church had been transformed through applying the principles of partnership, action-reflection and participation. Because Terry had put the church back in touch with its community; taken the time to learn the local culture; and allowed the needs of the poor neighbourhood to shape the agenda, it had gained a solid credibility as it began to explain how Jesus was relevant to the people and the needs of the area.

Because the community members were primarily non-book-orientated, the church realised that the people would have to 'see with their eyes' before they could be expected to 'perceive with their minds'. So they conceived a highly *visual* mission with plenty of drama and dancing. Pubs were central to the local people's sense of community, so – with fear and trembling – the church went inside the ale houses to hold highly-professional concerts. The locals just couldn't believe that Christians were going into some of the most notorious, drug-centred pubs in the whole of Toxteth! These adventurous forays were augmented by fun days, barbecues and colourful street parties. 'It was proclamation,' says Terry.

We took one step in Jesus' name into our community, and we invited the community to take one step towards Jesus. All we wanted to get across was, 'God is good, and you're not so bad after all.' That was the starting point, and we didn't raise expectations unrealistically. We looked at where we were at as a church, and the way the church fitted into the community. Seven years ago, we knew that we had to change 'within' before we could attract people from 'without'. Now, after seven years of sowing, we are starting to reap!

Willow Creek

Here, Terry Jones's church found their evangelism transformed when *they presented eternal truths in a manner that was relevant to contemporary culture.* They made their worship an offering to a God who wishes to see our churches grow, by drawing in the outsiders whom our normal worship often alienates. These 'outsiders' matter to God.

The Willow Creek church in Chicago made a similar decision. Instead of arranging its services in a way that would please its current members, it tried a 'seeker friendly' approach aimed at 'doing whatever was necessary to make a non-committed visitor feel most at home'. They acknowledged that the Gospel is often alarming and disconcerting when heard powerfully for the first time, and set out to make their services 'a safe place to pass on a dangerous message', says Paul Dakin of the Pioneer house church movement in the UK, who is sold on the principle. By addressing the needs of the typical non-Christian, the church tries to transform the outsider's thinking about God. The Gospel is presented in whatever clothing will make it most attractive to the local individual.

'The atmosphere of worship, the professional standards of the music and drama, and the modest biblical and practical teaching all impressed me,' says veteran evangelical leader John Stott of the Willow Creek approach. A typical service began as a presentation in which stories, songs and drama enfolded the common problems faced in everyday life, exposing the sense of failure, insecurity and uncertainty which underlie human experience. It showed how people try to live with the guilty legacy of previous actions, seeking for a way to be made clean again. Christ was presented as the answer, bringing God's mercy to a fallen world, but only once the question had been posed in a meaningful and relevant way. The uncommitted visitor is therefore able to participate more fully, and reflect more deeply, on the worship.

Exaltation, edification, evangelism and social action are seen as the foundations of the Christian life. Willow Creek's philosophy acknowledges that it is the responsibility of every church member to build relationships with the unchurched members of their community, and that it is the privilege of each believer to share a verbal witness as the opportunity arises. The building of relationships through a concern for social justice pays dividends in providing opportunities to present the Gospel, but a church needs to be ready to 'make itself presentable' – with culturally relevant worship – when outsiders become curious enough to attend a service.

Kingdom Coming!

The Tab had realised that, if it had exploited its impact on the community at too early a stage, the potential influx of new people would have found its unregenerate church life to be tedious and boring. We'll say this for the hundredth time: *The church itself had to change before it could expect to win its community for Christ.*

'A totally unchurched couple have started coming regularly for the past six weeks,' Terry explained in February 1997:

They say it's not at all how they had expected it to be, but infinitely better! They were loving every minute! We had broken the caricature of 'church', by letting them experience the presence of God in worship, without jumping on them or pressurising them to make a commitment for which they were not ready. At times, God's presence has been awesome and electric. The fellowship and atmosphere have been loving and warm. There is an essence of reality and honesty and life. There is such a cross-section of people, it feels like a family, reflecting every stage of growth.

Promises have been made by politicians to the people of Toxteth that have not been kept. The Tab has always been careful not to promise anything that it cannot deliver, but it has accepted people as they are and helped them to improve their lot in life. Its projects have given it the right to speak into the community. There is no superficiality, the community metaphorically 'gets its beef and potatoes', not just its tea and cucumber sandwiches. Now it's beginning to get a drink of living water to go with it!

The practices that have helped the Tab to make God's grace manifest in a local church context, to bring communities closer to the Kingdom of God, are effective the world over. The following list is quoted from a report produced by Tear Fund consultants Elizabeth Corrie and Simon Batchelor about a project in India; yet every single piece of good practice is equally applicable to the success in Liverpool of the Toxteth Tabernacle, and of the Frontline church:

- The vision of biblical holism that inspires and undergirds the work.
- Making transformation the major goal.
- The vision of the founders and leaders.
- The use of the Bible as an effective learning tool that can shape methodologies.
- Awareness of the benefits of a participatory approach to teaching and learning.
- The focus on learning through action and reflection.
- Good team work from dedicated staff.
- Links with the evangelical constituency and mission partners.

Parish Priest

Just up the road from the Tab, Robert Gallagher is faced with the dubious distinction of being the vicar of St Margaret's, the poorest parish of the poorest diocese in the Church of England. There are no far-reaching social action projects run from his church. Some of the needs of the people in his parish are different from those down at Terry Jones's end of Toxteth, and it is foolhardy to attempt to replicate schemes where they are simply not appropriate. Robert says:

> Christ didn't tell Nicodemus that he had to sell all he had; nor did he tell the rich young man that he had to be born again. He said the appropriate thing to each person he met; his message was not 'off the peg', it was tailor-made for the needs of each individual. He wasn't carrying the Gospel around like some script, nor did he have little bits of agenda in his head, wondering who to give them to; he said what was apt at each moment, through God's grace, as each occasion arose.

Rob feels that a lot of evangelicals have lost their faith because they have found that the old methods of bringing Jesus Christ into people's lives no longer seem to work. The days of altar calls and big rallies have passed. He feels that some Christian leaders have now become, effectively, social workers or project managers, as an alternative to being priests. The notion of lay empowerment often obscures the priest's true role in the community – it should be the members of the congregation who take on the management roles within any development project, he believes.

> Within six months of moving into this community, I was taken aside by a big black mama of a woman, who was very active and very well respected locally. She explained that the community didn't need me to be anything high and mighty. Neither did they need me to be 'one of the lads' like the previous vicar. 'And we certainly don't need another bloody social worker!' she said. What was really required, she explained, was for me to be 'in role' . . .

It took Rob a good deal of time to 'unpack' what the woman meant by the remark. It seemed that she expected Rob to be the parish priest, and for the church to be exactly that – a place of worship, and not a community centre. She was concerned that the church should not be confused with any other agency. The church and its members were there to deal with 'the God issues', and it was here that its true agenda was seen to lie – the agenda that the community wanted for it.

The King's Servant

Whereas Terry Jones had arrived in Toxteth to find a church composed of people from the suburbs who had lost touch with the community, Rob Gallagher found himself with a congregation of people who were very much still part of their local community, but who went to church as a way to escape from it! His is truly a church *of* the poor, and much of his work consists of comforting, supporting and empowering its members.

Some of the people Rob found in the church when he arrived were poor ex-students who stayed after university because the accommodation in the area was cheap. They looked on the church almost as a lifeboat, but left within twelve months of Rob's arrival. 'What am I left with? I'm left with people of the community who come to church. When the service is over, they go back and live in the community.'

It is as an individual Christian, who happens to be an ordained priest, that Rob moves amongst the non-churchgoing members of this rough neighbourhood, dealing with their 'God bits' for them. It's a tough and lonely task being God's servant, but it is truly the community's agenda for him, and he doesn't flinch from it. Like Terry he participates in the local community, his own life is reflective and prayerful, and he tries to help his parishioners to find space for their own reflection:

It's a long struggle. We're partnered by a very rich white middle-class church in St Albans, but they've fallen out with us at the moment, because we've told them that the good works they want to do with us are patronising! They want us to be better *social workers*. I see the church's role as making people better *human beings*, by letting them share in the worship and sacraments. When we've had our spiritual needs met, and had our souls touched, surely this will make us better family members.

It's the *process*, not the *activities*, that counts. The people in St Albans need to trust Rob's church to be able to meet the 'development' agenda of its own community, instead of imposing a condescending 'welfare' agenda on Toxteth residents who are then seen as 'victims'. Rob believes that the two parishes can learn from each other. Any financial contribution made by the well-to-do Christians would be best given to meet the Toxteth church's boring old running expenses, instead of trying to turn the congregation into social workers running unrealistic welfare projects that this particular community doesn't want!

Stories of the Street

Originally built by slave-owning white Liverpudlians as an Anglo-Catholic shrine, St Margaret's remarkably is now seen by the local people as being *their* church, where the traumas of births and deaths can be attended to, and where the deep questions of life and death can be asked without fear of ridicule. It is already a part of its neighbourhood; a community that is ready to tell Rob its stories.

The neighbourhood looks to the church to baptise their children, though they don't want to be long-term members. The parents make promises that they may not keep – at least not on the church's terms. 'I make the assumption that God is on their side, and that my role is to work within their own understanding of God, and to help them to deal with their own spirituality in their own terms,' says Rob.

Rob speaks of a woman who asked him to go round to her flat.

When he arrived, he noticed that the armchairs and settee were badly ripped. The woman explained that she had had a serious drug habit. She was a prostitute who sold her body on the streets to pay for her addiction. One day, she looked into the eyes of her eight-year-old daughter, and realised that she couldn't continue this way of life any longer, so she tried diligently to change her life. She found work and began to get her life back in order. But the neighbours came to believe that she must be pushing drugs, to have managed so well, so they called in the police. *It was the drug squad who had ruined her only furniture, by slitting it open to search for narcotics.* Rob remembers:

> We were sat on the torn-up settee and she was in tears. Then she turned to me and said, 'I am determined not to go back to drugs and prostitution, for the sake of my child. But I've got to *mark* this resolution in some way. When I look at my child, all I can think of is having my girl baptised. Will you do her?'
>
> My head was saying: What about church attendance? What about the vows? Does she know what they mean? Has she heard about Jesus? Will the child be confirmed afterwards? But my heart said simply 'Yes!' I'm not sure that the theology would have meant anything to her but, being well-versed in Scripture, the line that was going through my own mind – my 'gut feeling' – was: 'You are not far from the Kingdom of Heaven'.

Rob smiles. Who could dispute that she was taking giant leaps in the right direction?

The theology would have to come later. Rob considered that it was right, as Christ would have done, for the church initially to meet this woman at her point of need. That the ritual meant something to her, in her own terms, was – in this instance – more important than the stale crusts of strict doctrinal understanding. *Christianity lives first in the hearts of people, and not in fusty books of theology.*

Meaningful action would come first and, perhaps, the theological comprehension would follow later. But Rob would not make himself the woman's judge and jury. He performed the service, and has not seen the woman again. Perhaps she and her child will later come to know Christ in a more meaningful way. Perhaps not. But to push a loaded agenda on to her would probably have alienated her. Better to let her reflect on what baptism means to her, as a 'rite of passage', and to let the results of such reflection subtly transform her personal agenda. 'All I know is that the decision was right,' Rob affirms simply.

One of Rob's colleagues was murdered on his own doorstep by an irate parishioner, the previous year. This clergyman, Chris Gray, used to tell his colleagues an amusing story against himself. 'Why do you want to have your child baptised?' Chris asked a new mother who had come to him. 'To give thanks to God for the child,' she replied. Thinking about vows and church commitment, Chris probed deeper: 'Yes, but *why* do you want the child baptised?' Instead of giving a considered theological answer, the woman simply leaned forward in her chair, looked at Chris as though he was a couple of sandwiches short of a picnic, and asked: 'Are you *thick* or something?' She couldn't verbalise her reasons, but she had come to the vicar, because putting deep concepts into words was his job!

'Now that was the community *owning* its own theology, and taking it away from the church. It was using the church, on its own terms,' Rob Gallagher laughs.

A church may have all kinds of agendas about listening to the community, but in the end, it's in danger of only understanding what it *wants* to hear. For me, parish churches are part of the community anyway: we are the Church of England. In the finish, people will use the established church in their own way. It's enshrined in law that everyone in the parish can come to their church and demand weddings, baptisms and funerals; and the vicar can't say 'No'. The congregation uses the liturgy in its own way, too; not necessarily finding an intellectual understanding, they may simply 'catch the mystery'.

Regular churchgoers carry the community with them like

blooming great chains strapped around their ankles! They may sometimes be drunken womanisers, full of fury, but they come to church to resolve something; to say their prayers; to see what answers God has for them today. People come for their own theological reasons that, sometimes, the church doesn't understand.

Rob and Terry's approaches are different, but the underlying values are similar:

- The process is more important than specific activities.
- Self-help is better than welfare 'service provision'.
- Love, care and compassion are essential.
- The long haul is the only way.
- Reflection is vital in providing opportunities for change.

God's Hairdresser

All human life is present in Rob's parish church, just as it is in the Toxteth Tab's coffee shop. Neither is 'better' or more 'correct' than the other. Each is appropriate in terms of addressing community needs, and responding to the agendas of local people. Ask the community whether their agenda is one of *evangelism* or *social care*, and you risk receiving the same response that Chris Gray received from the woman wanting her child baptised . . .

It's not justice or freedom these people need, its God's *mercy*. They know they can't 'do it on their own'. They are under no delusions about their own lack of righteousness, because the whole area runs on a black market economy. Rob's dad was a tailor who often found himself dealing in cloth 'knocked off' from the docks, supplied by people who wanted to look like Duke Ellington or Katherine Hepburn, but usually ended up more like Al Capone. Double standards abound. The people know it but lack the financial wherewithal to get out of the trap. God bestows his unmerited favour wherever there is both true turning away from wrongdoing, and an acceptance that heaven is a free gift which is not for sale in any market, black or otherwise.

God's grace is manifest on the streets of Toxteth, as the stories above testify. Rob says:

> We've got a bit tabloidish about God's grace. It's not cheap. People don't get changed overnight. Even Saint Paul, after his Damascus Road experience, was still a hard-bitten tough guy filled with determination – only now, instead of killing Christians, he was going out to evangelise Asia Minor! The Church should not be surprised if, when it stays with community, it meets with wilderness. Nor should it be surprised, if it stays with community even longer, when it meets its Good Friday. Isn't this where the church should be?

Standing outside his fortress-like vicarage in the darkness of a winter's evening, Rob points out the burnt ruins just opposite – still lying derelict from the Toxteth riots fifteen years earlier. He talks of a barber who is an evangelical Christian, in the heart of the riot area, whose church frequently urges him to get on to the streets and to give out tracts. The barber always replies that his hairdressing *is* his ministry. All the local gangsters come to his shop to have their hair cut. It's one of the few acts in our culture which allows people to be touched; so here are all these local hard men having their heads stroked by a Christian barber, as he cuts their hair!

With this degree of intimacy, friendship develops, and these brigands begin to talk to him. As he leads them in reflection, they start to struggle with the ethics of their unsavoury professions – drug-dealing, gun-running, pimping – and to address their 'God bits'. Some of these people are gradually amassing money for the benefit of their children. They tell their barber that, once they are into their thirties and forties, they will step sideways out of the black economy and buy legitimate businesses with their ill-gotten gains. Laughing at the absurdity, Rob comments:

> This is just like the story that Jesus told about the unjust steward!

There, in the ambiguity of the situation, within the darkness of the place, there is the Gospel light! Show me a prostitute who is not on the streets to earn a better life for herself and her family. No one else is going to help them. Over there are the men crying into their beers, praying for ease from their pain. You have to wait long enough, and to be in the position – either literally or metaphorically – to massage them, before you begin really to hear their stories.

Because you *do* wait long enough – and because you baptise their babies and bury their dead – this intimacy not only allows you to hear why they do the terrible things they do, it also begins to enable *them* to see *themselves as they truly are*, warts and all. With self-understanding comes reflection, and they begin to see the God element in their existence – as a way that they can follow, other than the old way that has screwed up and laid waste their precious lives.

Perform one good act for one individual and the whole family knows about it. The news spreads like wildfire through the streets of the neighbourhood, and the whole district identifies with it, *becoming* a community in the process. It's not the church's job to turn them all into Christians, or to hope that people will fall sideways into the church through using its social facilities; the church's job is to wait with hope, and sacrificially to follow Christ. When people begin to ask questions, further reflection can begin to direct them towards a merciful God's saving grace. *The role of each Christian in the local community needs to be such that it deliberately and intentionally encourages people outside the Church to reflect on what is happening in their lives.*

Like John Matthews up in Glasgow, Rob Gallagher and Terry Jones have found that subtle theological nuances seem less important when suddenly faced with the carnage of real people who are emotionally haemorrhaging under the hustle and bustle of their tragic lives. Christians need to think through the issues in advance, so that they don't end up *devising* their theology 'on the hoof'. But it's best not to have your theological script so set in stone that there is no space for *revising* it to 'play' in the toughest of practical situations. At its best, good theology provides space for improvisation: it should be a Hendrix guitar solo, not a drum machine programme.

Jesus wept. We need to, as well.

Questions and Exercises

- What would *you* do if confronted with the prostitute who wanted her child baptised?
- Do you agree with Rob that the story of the Unjust Steward (Luke 16:1–8) speaks into the situation in Toxteth?
- Look at the list of eight points of good practice (it appears after the Toxteth Tab section). How many of those points would apply in your own church situation?
- Look carefully at your answers to question 3. *Now, what are you going to do about* it?
- Meditate on the meaning of God's Kingdom, praying for its significance in your own life.

8

Free From Debt

Mrs Robinson is typical of many single parents. She was a very capable person, but her life fell apart when her partner left. Her inadequate income of $600 per month has meant that she has run up $10,000 of debt. She has a heroin habit that she feeds through being in debt to a loan shark in the project housing of downtown Los Angeles where she lives. 'I'll lend you $100 today,' says the shark, 'but for collateral, I want your welfare book and a copy of your front door key. I will meet you when your next welfare payment is due on Thursday, when you will pay me $150 back. And remember, I've got your front door key . . .'

The impact on Mrs Robinson's attitudes and her perceptions of Christianity – *if a local Christian now stands between her and the loan shark to recover the benefit book, and then pays for the locks to be changed on her doors* – will be truly life-transforming. The Church can only be effective in this situation by taking such drastic measures. To invite Mrs Robinson to attend a family service at her local church, or even to arrange for Mrs Robinson to receive debt counselling, are totally inadequate responses.

A Christian becoming involved must help to solve the problem that is actually there – not offer a purely long-term solution to a problem that is immediately pressing, or a spiritual diversion from a very real economic calamity where the client's physical safety is under threat! If you take the wrong action, someone – perhaps you! – will end up in hospital. Get it right, and you can then lead Mrs Robinson in a reflection that will probably turn her life around, and result in her making a real and lasting commitment to the Lord Jesus.

Indebted

In a similar situation in the UK, John Kirkby, a Christian with experience in the credit industry, knew that if the woman voluntarily made a realistic offer, the creditors would be foolish to decline. It is important, in these situations, that the full scope of the economic disaster is revealed – with nothing held back. On her behalf, he offered her creditors a repayment plan that would entail her making regular payments to a total of £7,000 in complete satisfaction of debts totalling £21,000, and all the creditors agreed.

This was not an act of generosity on the part of the creditors, who knew well that under the various laws that regulate loans of money, this was the best that they could expect. Had they declined, they ran the risk that the debtor would declare herself bankrupt, and the creditors would receive only a few pounds. The sense that 'someone else knows my circumstances and can do something about it' took an enormous weight off the woman's shoulders. The heroin habit had simply been a means of coping with the stress, and she was soon rehabilitated. Shortly afterwards, simply through the impact on her life of the comfort and advice she had received, the woman became a Christian.

At the end of the day, this is not just about 'debt counselling', *it's about setting someone free.* The woman was given hope, that tomorrow can be different from yesterday. It happened, not by accident, but because the debt counsellor's church supported the initiative prayerfully and financially; twelve members of the congregation had volunteered to conduct follow-up work with the project's clients. Now the woman is witnessing to other single mums in the same situation that she used to be in, testifying that 'these Christians really helped me in my need'.

Volunteers are not 'merely a substitute for paid staff' – a second-best option when there is no funding available. They are the heart and soul of any community project! When a luncheon club for elderly people, that had run for five years with a team of twenty-five volunteers, phoned UK Action wanting a grant to employ a qualified food hygiene specialist, they were told, 'No, you can't have a salary to employ an outside professional, but we will pay you to send ten of your volunteers on a course to get the relevant qualification – and it will only cost a tenth as much money!' This is true participation, that is highly developmental. You can make a difference yourself; you don't have to 'call in the experts' to do the job, though you may need their advice and professional skills.

How to Get into Debt . . .

'There are several common ways in which people get into trouble with money,' says Keith Tondeur, Director of Credit Action, a Christian organisation that has moved beyond simple debt counselling to embrace an educational and development role. Keith adds:

The prime one is that people don't budget, so they don't really know where their money goes. Time and time again if you are counselling somebody, they may say they are spending £60 per week on rent, £60 on food, £10 on gas, £10 on electric and £120 on 'miscellaneous'. When I ask, 'What's that?' they say, 'I don't know. That's what I get paid and that's what's gone.' Another problem is that of priorities and people not really knowing what they are wanting to do. They think their priorities are, say, the children's clothing – but they spend far more on cheese rolls or other everyday things.

Obviously the use of credit is a major factor. People take on agreements left, right and centre, and then realise that actually they may have six or seven different agreements that are costing £1,500 a month. Maybe they can afford one, but they can't afford six.

And of course you've still got the big problems of unexpected unemployment and, in particular, the problem of the people who are unsuccessfully self-employed, which I think is an increasing situation. There are no more 'jobs for life'; most people will face redundancy at least once in their lifetime, or at the very least will have to learn new skills. But products like mortgages, insurance and pensions have not changed. They are still products for life, so you can take out a mortgage for twenty-five years, which is a major long-term commitment. There is a great wodge of people who are heavily reliant on future income to pay off their existing debts. *In many cases their current debt is far more than a year's income.* Many people are horrified and that's why they don't like adding it all up – they may admit they owe £500 here and £1000 there but if you actually say to them, 'Well that means you owe £15,000 in total,' it makes people feel terrible. It's the *accumulation* of credit which is obviously a major factor, if something does go wrong.

The consumer society is a problem because of the instant gratification it encourages. There is an immense pressure, even sometimes in Christian circles, to be wearing the right sort of 'gear' to go to the right sort of places. Those sorts of pressure are enormous and, because many people can't afford to pay cash any more, they are having to borrow to 'keep up with the Joneses', even though the Joneses are famously struggling to keep up with them! People get reckless, and push up to their limit as far as they can possibly get away with; usually, the first time you exceed your credit limit, the credit card company will send you a nice letter saying, 'Since you can't stay within your existing limit, we've increased it for you!' A few months later, the nasty letter comes, saying, 'Pay up or else!'

'Some advice bureaux take the problem over; write to the creditors; and get some agreements, or maybe arrange a consolidated loan,' says Keith. 'But I think in six months' or a year's time, they would be in the same position – because they have tried to put a sticking plaster over an open wound.' They haven't been trained to use money properly. What they really need to know is, 'How did I get into this situation in the first place?' They either haven't got enough income or they are overspending. *In most cases it's overspending.*

We are not taught the basics of money education in our schools and colleges. Consequently:

- People fail to keep in contact with their creditors.
- If they do, they forget to keep copies of correspondence.
- They don't check out their benefits position with the DSS.
- They don't keep their close family members informed.
- They don't separate their priority debtors from the non-urgent.
- They don't keep proper statements.

Instead, they bury their heads in the sand; they refuse to open bills; they ignore court summonses; they waste money on non-essential items; and they make rash promises that they know they can't fulfil. They are intimidated by debt collectors (even from so-called respectable firms) and the social stigma attached – what the neighbours overhear on the doorstep and so on!

In 1997, Credit Action counselled a couple aged twenty-four and twenty-five who had debts between them of £140,000. The credit system in Britain means that the more you borrow the more you *can* borrow – rather than lenders saying, 'Now hang on, enough is enough.' And of course the temptation is enormous.

Taking Action

If we are not budgeting, we are not handling our money sensibly. If we are buying things we don't need, then we are being very bad stewards and we are wasting money at a time when there are millions of people in the world who are at starvation levels. This is one of the big topics that the Christian Church has not faced up to at all in the West, probably because some Christians feel guilty if they have got money, and others feel very guilty if they haven't got money, so it's far easier to pretend that there isn't a problem and not speak about it at all. Keith says:

I think money is one of the most talked-about subjects in the Bible so it's obviously an area of major biblical teaching. And you only have to think about how long in a normal day you are earning money, spending it, saving it, giving it or worrying about it, to realise that it is a major issue that affects most of us *on a day-to-day basis*. If we as Christians are not allowing our faith to affect the way we handle our money in any way, shape or form – apart from a little bit of giving – we are falling far short of what we could and should be doing.

Debt is now being named as the number one cause of marriage breakdown in over 70 per cent of cases. It is a serious issue. Somehow our society says, 'The one who dies with the most toys is the winner,' or that 'Money helps you to obtain everything, even love.' We are all so busy and at the same time so lonely, which is a complete contradiction; but that seems to be the sort of society we are in.

How can people in their local churches help people with debt problems?
'Some of the bigger churches can get together and form little debt counselling groups,' suggests Keith. 'That's what happened, for example, in Cardiff where they have now moved into the High Street, away from the church environment.' Credit Action has got a free helpline (0800 591084), produces a wide range of material, and offers regular training days for churches and individual Christians who would like to become involved in this work.

We need to think about our church notice boards, and what we put on them. Yes, it's important to know about the times of services, but can we also please put down, 'If you need help, come and talk to us; or if you don't want to speak to us, here's the number of Relate, Samaritans, or CAB.' Have that on a major notice board in the High Street as people pass, and it's a tremendous service to the community – especially to someone at the end of their tether.

I had a lady call me up last Friday and she said, 'I just needed to talk to you personally, because three months ago somebody gave me your book *Say Goodbye to Debt* – on the day I had decided to drive off a cliff! If I hadn't got your book, I wouldn't be here to talk to you today.

A Feast of Jubilees

It's not just individuals who are enslaved by their economic conditions, *whole countries are in the same position.* They are in need of a Jubilee, when all their debts can get written off, freeing them from the credit trap. If an animal is caught in a trap, one thing is certain: the trap didn't get there by itself, it was put there by a hunter. So when the poor get caught in the poverty trap, it is right to ask: 'Who put the trap there in the first place?'

The International Monetary Fund (IMF) and the World Bank are international lending agencies who lend money to countries that are experiencing financial difficulties. Rather as clearing banks, credit card companies and loan sharks do with their personal borrowers, if a country cannot repay the loan, a further loan is made so that repayment instalments and interest can be met. If you can't repay the original loan, they make you borrow some more!

The impact of this policy is felt most keenly by the poor people, who find their governments skimping on basic amenities in order to keep up with loan repayments that seem to get larger and larger each year. Each year, the Third World pays the West three times more in debt repayments than it receives in aid. Both Peru and Zambia pay around a third of their national income every year on interest and loan repayments. In consequence, public spending cuts eat away at education and healthcare. Zambia's debt works out at £479 per head of the population in 1995, while the Gross National

Product is only £253 per head! The result: 86 per cent of the population live in poverty, unable to afford food and essentials. More than 20 per cent of the children die before their fifth birthday, and adult life expectancy is only 45.4 years. Africa, as a whole, spends four times as much on debt repayments at it does on healthcare. *And this oppression is all perfectly 'legal'.*

The Bible is not silent about such injustice: 'Woe to those who make unjust laws, to those who issue oppressive decrees, to deprive the people of their rights and rob my oppressed people of justice' (Isaiah 10:1, 2). Psalm 94:20 condemns those who 'frame mischief by statute' (RSV).

Essentially, poor countries have gone bankrupt; but there is none of the provision for them that there would be for a company or individual who goes bankrupt and is thereby protected from creditors. Since the late 1970s, various plans have been laid by Western governments for *some* of the debt eventually to be cancelled, but this partial remission is inevitably tied in with schemes to restructure the remainder of the debt in ways that maintain repression. Many countries have had to switch agricultural production from food crops to narcotics, which generate greater income, in order to service their debts. For example, 40 per cent of Bolivia's workforce depend on the drugs trade for a living. (Statistics from *The Debt Cutter's Handbook*.) In consequence, the country's poorest population is drawn to the brink of starvation, while the cities of the West are flooded with dangerous and illegal drugs!

Ronald Sider explores this political injustice at length, concluding that – like Zacchaeus in the Gospels – the Western world needs to repent and to make restitution. The Church can help, and many Christians are already leading the way. The Evangelical Fellowship of Zambia encourages the promotion of relief and development, and has helped thousands of families through income-generating schemes. 'In seeking to deal with world debt, it is not just economies with which we are dealing, but a spirit of greed and power,' says Roger Forster. The only solution is the kind of Jubilee we saw in chapter two.

A Biblical Pattern

But it's very negative to concentrate purely on how to offer practical help to oppressed people in dire financial need. We also need to arrive at a proper biblical perspective on the use of money, and to see the implications for each individual's lifestyle. We need to 'take the plank out of our own eye' first.

The Bible sees personal poverty mainly in terms of economic deprivation, often caused by oppression. Those who are rich are often the people who, like Oliver Twist, are still hungry for more – and who do not care who has to suffer in order for them to live an extravagant lifestyle. These oppressors, the people with money and power, are often guilty not only of injustice – refusing to pay a decent wage to the workers whose labours produce the affluence – but also of idolatry, in exercising a devotion to the accumulation and retention of money that amounts to worship.

Scripture advocates just personal dealings, and condemns rich oppressors with a fearful vehemence:

> Now listen, you rich people, weep and wail because of the misery that is coming upon you . . . Look! The wages you failed to pay the workmen who mowed your fields are crying out against you. The cries of the harvesters have reached the ears of the Lord Almighty. You have lived on earth in luxury and indulgence. You have fattened yourselves in the day of slaughter. (James 5:1,4,5.)

The Bible is rich with such condemnation! Here are some more references that you could explore: Exod. 22:21–4, 23:6; Deut. 15:13–15; 1 Sam. 2:2–8; Pss. 14:31, 19:17, 72:1–4, 146; Prov. 14:31, 19:17; Isa. 1:10–17, 3:14–25, 58:3–8; Jer. 5:26–9, 22:13–19; Ezek. 16:49, 50; Amos 6:4, 7, 7:4; Luke 4:18, 19; 6:20–5, 14:12–14; 2 Cor. 8:9; Heb. 13:1–3; Jas. 2:1–7; 1 John 3:17, 18. And this is only the tip of the iceberg. The Scriptures attach particular distaste to the practices of failing to pay adequate wages; failure to pay wages on time; indulging in ostentatious living; and hoarding wealth such that it performs no useful function. But there is another side to the coin . . .

Wealthy in Wisdom

Probably the most misquoted verse in the whole of Scripture is 'Money is the root of all evil'; it should, of course, be '*the love* of money . . .' There is nothing wrong with wealth, *per se*, for there are many wealthy men in Scripture who walked close to God's heart. Noah couldn't have afforded to build his ark if he had been poor. Abraham had large flocks, which he handed down through Isaac and Jacob. Joseph, as the Vizier of an Egyptian Pharaoh, was the second most important person in the land, and he would have shared in the great prosperity which his economic forethought brought to Egypt in the wake of famine. And King David was 'not short of a bob or two'!

The apostles, though none were fabulously wealthy, numbered several with considerable business income. Peter and John's fishing business was sufficiently affluent to employ hired help. As a former tax collector, Matthew could have had a sizeable nest egg by the time he met up with Jesus. The fact that Paul was born a Roman citizen suggests that his family were affluent – to become a Roman citizen cost 'a big price' (Acts 22:28). Many of Christ's other followers were hardly paupers; Joseph of Arimathea owned a rock tomb, the Rolls Royce of burial places, while Nicodemus could afford to buy seventy-five pounds of spice to anoint Christ's body (John 19:39). Luke would have found the medical profession to be very lucrative, and the family of Mary and Martha possessed a jar of ointment that was 'worth a year's wages' (John 12:5).

The distinctive is that all these people used their wealth *wisely, and justly, for the good of other members of the community.* These people didn't hoard their wealth, nor were they vulgar and ostentatious in the way they used it. (A sound attitude is to think of money as something to be *used*, rather than something to be *spent*.) They were judicious with their use of time, too. Saint Paul is rightly revered as a great missionary, but wrongly viewed as simply a man who won souls for Christ. His proclamation evangelism worked side by side with his social evangelism, addressing practical everyday needs as a witness to the values of God's Kingdom.

He devoted much of his time to raising funds for oppressed Jewish Christians amongst gentile congregations. He demonstrated that Christians from one location were intended to share their wealth amongst other believers, irrespective of intervening political or cultural boundaries. In AD 46, for example, believers at Antioch (in Asia Minor) gave 'each according to his ability' (Acts 11:29) to those Christians adversely affected by the famine in Palestine. This economic sharing is alluded to repeatedly in Paul's letters (Rom. 15:26–8; 1 Cor. 16:1–4). Paul's account of his meeting with the apostles in Jerusalem is quite staggering. He records the mandate that these great Christian leaders gave to him: '*All they asked was that we should continue to remember the poor, the very thing I was eager to do*' (Gal. 2:10).

To free people from guilt and poverty, it is necessary for us to share resources, and to live a simple lifestyle. Tom Sine, in *The Mustard Seed Conspiracy*, cites one example of good stewardship:

Hilda is a seventy-two-year-old Jewish Christian who lives in West Germany. Her home has become a centre of loving reconciliation that seems to draw people from everywhere. On any given day, one can find an unlikely assortment of people there: a young Arab studying theology in Berlin to prepare himself to be a pastor of an Arab Christian church in a strongly Muslim village in Israel. A young woman from Lima, Peru, who found her way back to God in Hilda's home only weeks before.

It's an exemplary lifestyle.

Let's Get Started!

Now it's your turn! Leave the television off; take tea and toast instead of a main meal; put aside the newspaper; and let the carpet get by without being vacuumed today. Spend time, instead, reading through some Scripture verses. There is a list earlier in this chapter that will get you started. See how many more references you can find to the wise use of resources. A trawl through Amos will gather you a rich dividend about poverty, injustice and oppression; and naturally, Christ had much to say on the subject – begin with the Sermon on the Mount (Matt. 5–7). Then pick up the newspaper again, and look through some of the news stories; try to find examples of where these Scriptures have keen applications in those practical situations.

Next, go through your wardrobe and remove any clothing you haven't worn in the past year; and there's probably something in there that's now several sizes too small for you – you'll never fit into those trousers again! It's time to prune your record/tape/CD collection, too. Be firm with yourself; anything you haven't played in the last twelve months has got to go! Go through your home and find which household items you have not used for the past year; there's probably a whole heap taking up space at the back of a cupboard somewhere. Can you really justify keeping these items?

Find out where the next car boot sale is near you; sell all those unused items; and give the money to the poor. There is a list of organisations at the back of the book who can recommend worthy projects that will gladly receive your tithes, or you can put the money aside for development work in your own locality. But we mustn't lose sight of the redemption theme that runs through the Bible; anything that you really can't bear to be parted from can be 'redeemed' by substituting an item of similar value. Legitimate collections, kept as a hobby, can be saved; but ask yourself whether the collection exists purely for your own pleasure, or whether others derive pleasure from sharing in it. *Be tough on yourself!*

A Biblical Lifestyle

John Wesley argued that Christians should give away all but the bare necessities of life. He practised what he preached: the hundreds of pounds per year that he received from sales of his books were given away, and he survived on just £30 per annum – though it went a lot further in those days! Ronald Sider suggests a graduated tithing system, which entails giving away 10 per cent of a 'base rate' assessed as an income that permits reasonable comfort, but not luxury. At various levels of income above the base rate, a larger proportion is given away; above a certain level, everything is given away.

The hallmarks of a truly biblical approach to wealth are: a sustainable lifestyle; a rejection of excess luxury; and a rejection of any expenditure made solely for pride or status. We really shouldn't spend money simply because it is there in our bank account. Nor should we surround ourselves with 'trappings' of success. It's fine to spend money on recreation and hobbies, within sound limits. Occasional celebrations are acceptable, but to dine out excessively and over-frequently smacks of worldliness. We need to concern ourselves with the needs of others.

Set yourself a 'target area' of 5–8 neighbours in whose welfare you are going to take a personal interest. Perhaps you should pick your two neighbours either side of your house, and the three houses directly opposite. If you live in a flat, you might want to choose the neighbours on the same landing, and perhaps the flats above and below. Begin by praying for these people regularly. Ask God to show you their needs. Who are the poorest? Are there any one-parent families, elderly people, or families with young children who are struggling to make ends meet?

Start simply. Next time you go shopping, purchase one loaf more than you need. You're not going to be able to use it yourself, so you can quite honestly call on your neighbours – commencing with the ones you perceive to be the neediest – and say, 'I seem to have too much bread. Can I give you this loaf? It seems a pity to see it go to waste.' A couple of weeks later, buy an extra pint of milk, select a different neighbour, and repeat the process.

Now, this is not *community development* in itself, but it will enable you to make contact in a beneficial way with people in your own local community; you are beginning to break down barriers; you start to become part of the solution instead of part of the problem! Give your neighbour a chance to reciprocate, perhaps by asking to borrow tools or gardening implements. If a particular neighbour seems to be in particular financial need, pop some banknotes into an envelope (in consultation with your spouse, if you are married) – perhaps you could add a note saying 'this comes to you as a gift, in the name of Jesus' – nip out after dark, and drop it through their letterbox. *Let your own prosperity be a blessing to others.*

St Augustine pointed out that the riches which God gives to his people are only like rings – tokens and pledges of devotion and commitment – they are not the beloved himself. True change comes not simply from casting aside old habits, it comes from the celebration of a new lifestyle. *Are you ready to make the difference in your community?*

The Chains of Wealth

When Ram Gidoomal visited those Mumbai slums, as described back in chapter four, he found that the Christian workers there were praying that we in the West would be released from *our* poverty! They meant that we never seem to think that we have *enough*; 'enough', for people in the West, always seems to be defined as 'a little more than I have at the moment'. We're never satisfied! Our wants are greater than our needs, and poverty means never having as much as you think you need!

At one time, Ram was earning enormous sums of money, running a Scotland-based company, part of a multi-national group with 7,000 employees. He wasn't simply on track to become a millionaire; he was well on his way to being a businessman with an earning potential of a million pounds *each year*! To be freed from his own 'poverty' – the relentless cycle of always wanting more than he had – he had to begin to take some tough decisions:

When I took up the job in Scotland, the group Chief Executive wanted me to live in a *castle* – after all, it was within my expense budget and would certainly look good to potential business contacts. But my family – all five of us – actually lived in a two-bedroom rented bungalow, because we knew that the rent we paid to the missionary couple who owned it would help them to survive financially as missionaries in Zimbabwe. I arrived home from work each day in my Mercedes, and went into a bungalow that was worth less than my car. It was ridiculous; the entire street looked on in disbelief every time I did it!

The issue, however, is not one of where we live nor even how much we have. Despite the life I was leading as a rich Christian, I was still *poor*, because I wasn't released fully to the role into which God was calling me. When I talked to those Christians in Mumbai, I realised that *they* were released from *their* poverty – they had no luxuries, but they didn't need them. They weren't like so many Western Christians (who apparently haven't read Luke 12:16–21) saying: 'I'd love to be of more use in the church, but I have my mortgage to think about. I'm only earning £45,000 per year, and I don't know how I'm going to manage . . .'

I knew of an unmarried young Christian with an important job in the city, and a beautiful house in the suburbs. He came to me and explained that he felt called into Christian ministry, but he wasn't sure how he would manage to cope financially. So we sat down together and worked out his net worth. His house was valued at £200,000, though he still had a £60,000 mortgage outstanding. So I pointed out that he could have £140,000 capital by selling the house, and – with interest rates of 10 per cent at that time – he could earn himself £14,000 per annum simply by putting the money in a bank. If he then moved to South Asia as a missionary, that income would make him a very wealthy man indeed – the average annual income over there was only £1,000 per annum. I explained that he would be a released pair of hands with a huge network, who could suddenly start to make things happen! But he turned away sad.

Even a man £140,000 above destitution feared for his financial security . . . 'It was like the rich young man whom Christ instructed should sell all his possessions; even though *this* man could keep the money, he just couldn't bring himself to give up the security of his profession. *Now THAT is the poverty trap in which so many Western Christians are caught!'*

But it's one from which Ram himself was determined to escape. Like certain fishermen from Galilee who gave up their jobs to devote themselves full-time to God's work, Ram took the inevitable step of extricating himself from the family business.

'I'm Set Free!'

When I gave up my own job, people gasped, 'But you're giving up the potential of a seven-figure salary, Ram!' I replied that I couldn't see the point of amassing more and more money that I couldn't find time to spend. I wanted to be released! As soon as I took that mental, physical, spiritual and emotional step – in consultation with my wife and our three children – I sat down and asked myself what I would really like to do. Bible college was the first step. I'm a convert from Hinduism, so I wanted to learn more about the Bible.

Here was the exciting potential of release and liberation through being made to see other forms of wealth – real wealth, in Christ. At a church in Switzerland, where I lived at one time, I knew a Norwegian couple for whom God wonderfully provided. They were evangelists and church workers – he drove a truck to make ends meet – but they were *released* people, living released lives. I was challenged by Tom Sine's book *The Mustard Seed Conspiracy*, and over the years I must have bought hundreds of copies to give away: Tom Sine says freeze your expenditure and your income; cancel your meetings and totally free your diary. One by one, I resigned from all my committees. I had two cars, so I sold one – my Mercedes! For two years, I used public transport. We were prepared to sell our house – we are not 'attached' to it – but eventually decided to hang on to it because it would be useful for hospitality.

Notice that Ram's decision was not taken hastily. It came about gradually, through prayer; the challenge of other Christians' lives; the inequalities he saw; and through sound Christian teaching. The Scriptures were the clincher, particularly Romans 12:2: 'Do not conform any longer to the pattern of this world, but be transformed by the renewing of your mind. Then you will be able to test and approve what God's will is – his good, pleasing and perfect will.'

The Rich Fruits of Evangelism

'We use the word "evangelism" as if it means something you do without social action, without care and without compassion; as though it were some undiluted words that flow from one person to another, and the other person suddenly says they are converted,' Ram exclaims. 'I wish it were that simple! When we talk about evangelism and sharing the Gospel, for me, it is the fullness of a holistic approach.' Many of the churches in India are ultra-traditional. To bring Hindus into a Bible study and to convert them to Christ is fine, but they still don't have drinking water, the children still die of disease and malnutrition, and the wives are still beaten up by their husbands. *The spectre of poverty can only effectively be removed by transforming the community.* Ram explains:

> Traditional forms of evangelism are often very shallow. In the Asian community, I've seen nine out of ten 'converts' who put their hands up at evangelistic meetings slip back. But in my own family, I have seen more than fifteen people come to Christ when they saw the Gospel as more than just words – as a total, living, vibrant experience.

Society is changing, and there is now so much information available to sift through before making up one's mind. One Zoroastrian colleague felt he couldn't make a commitment to Christ, because he didn't even know enough about his *own* faith to know whether Christianity was a viable option. So I sent him to Zoroastrian House in London, with the names of Zoroastrian experts to consult. They spent a year making their own investigations, then they phoned me and asked to come and stay with me. I knew at that point that they wanted to make a commitment to Christ, and I was proved correct!

We need to keep discipling and assuring people. Through social care, we are breaking down barriers and building bridges; now my confidence is that across those bridges, the Gospel we proclaim by our lives will reach these people.

'Take My Yoke'

When an earthquake devastated Maharashtra in India, in 1993, a group of theology students went out to try to help. 'What can we do?' they asked. 'Go out into the fields and harvest the crops!' they were told. The local people were too busy trying to put their lives back together, but if the crop didn't come in soon, it would wither and rot in the fields; then there would be no food for the winter, nothing to sell to maintain economic stability, and no seed to plant the next year. The people would face further disaster and many would starve. But the students wanted to be pastors and evangelists, not farmers. They refused.

Ram Gidoomal was asked by the Indian High Commissioner to make a response to the earthquake disaster. God provided an opportunity to raise funds on GMTV, in partnership, to construct a hospital in the area. £500,000 was raised, to build a Christian-run hospital serving a population of 140,000 people, providing a powerful Christian witness in an area that had not previously known one. No Christians were killed in the earthquake, not because of God's providence, but for a more mundane reason – there were no Christians living in the area, and no churches to be destroyed, because the area has never known any Christian ministry. *Well, there is one now!*

'Christians have been pioneers in responding to the acute social needs in India over the past 200 years,' says theologian Robin Thompson, Director of *Satya Bhavan* (The House of Truth). 'The

Christian Church in India has always been concerned with reaching out in compassion, and protesting against injustice. Only where there is no clear social need has the Church turned to a strictly vocal witness.'

The institutionalised witness of schools and hospitals might have been in danger of atrophying, were it not for new responses to old problems that had previously gone unaddressed, such as the plight of children with special needs. Nothing was being done for those with cerebal palsy and acute learning difficulties, which many parents tried to cover up for fear of shame and disgrace. A ministry to street children in Mumbai – partly financed by Christmas Cracker – began to thrive during the mid-1990s.

When the Gospel comes to Asians through Indian evangelists, it has the right cultural background, but it also has the track record of all the schools and hospitals that Christians have been building for 200 years. Suddenly, it all falls into place for them! Robin says:

In India, family life is so strong that, if you're going to be homeless, you land on the street as a family. In Britain, in that situation, the family will break up with one or two people ending up on the street and the children taken into care. The Asian-style extended family offers a much bigger structure, and greater security. In the West, if husband and wife have a problem, there's often no one to turn to; not so in India, where it is a matter of pride for family members to help one another.

There is a sobering lesson there for people in the West. *Families and relationships are our real treasure, not the money we have in the bank.* God works through churches, voluntary organisations, families and individuals, but seldom through banks! We need to waken from the Western dream with its secular agenda, and greet the dawn of God's emerging Kingdom.

'Spare a Few Coppers . . . ?'

The annals of missionary history are scattered with examples of people stepping out with no resources and having God provide those resources, and these are the models at the back of many Christians' minds. But we have to be careful when money is being 'prayed in'; dare we spend it *before* it arrives? Is it ever right to borrow money?

There's a world of difference between stepping out to do a work that is possible without resources (which might not last long without resources, and which could be done much better *with* resources); and spending money you haven't got (for something that needs extensive resources) in the full knowledge that you haven't got it. This is where many Christians are misled; *they do the latter rather than the former.* They borrow money from other projects for the new one, hoping that people will see it work, get fired up and support it. Beware! At the time of writing, there is a court case pending against one Christian who did just this, and 'borrowed' money illegally from one charity to support another. It is best to set up a work which can run with very few resources, to start it small and then to 'grow it'.

God is waiting to hear our prayers; like the Spice Girls, he is constantly asking, 'Tell me what you want, what you really, really want!' and we should be praying for the resources that we need to perform his will (and not for our personal prosperity). But God begins to work when *we* begin to work; we should be looking to raise any 'seed money' that is needed from our own resources, perhaps through the methods mentioned earlier in this chapter.

There will usually come a need for funding if local community projects are to be free from debt. But funding isn't simply about money; you also need a fund of ideas, a fund of stories and a fund of experience. Jennie Collins, International Director of Tear Fund, says:

Overseas partners give us fuel for support; not just the stories but the whole situations, which we use for publicity purposes. If they didn't exist, we couldn't get any support, so we wouldn't exist either; so we're very dependent upon the poor. People go overseas 'to help the poor' but they find that they themselves get changed as much as the people they have gone to help. The poor have helped *them* in return.

Many projects throughout the world give their *expertise* to other projects in other parts of the world; there is a mutual sharing. To transform a community requires people to work together for a common cause. 'The issue is one of relationship, you have to build a development relationship in order to explore the issue of transformation,' says Jennie. 'You need to take time exploring the relationship, taking time to understand just what the relationship *is* that is there.'

In 1994, Tear Fund had a dip in its income. It didn't cut its funding to overseas partners, but it had to stagger payments; it couldn't give six months' money at one time, but one month or three months at a time. Seeing the problem, churches in poor parts of the world *gave money to Tear Fund*, in order that it could be redistributed to those who were even worse off than themselves! A church in Fiji, for example, raised funds to send a worker to Sudan.

There's a story of a newly-appointed Nigerian bishop who was preparing to travel the world to tell people of the plight of his countrymen, and to try to raise funds for his church. Working down an alphabetical list of the world's nations, he decided that America, Australia and Austria seemed good places to try to raise money. When he came to Bangladesh on the list, he was ready to pass over on the grounds that this poor developing country would not have money that it could spare. But a Tear Fund partner stopped him and explained that the churches in Bangladesh were actually very generous in their giving to people 'worse off than themselves'. Could any country be much worse off than Bangladesh? Here indeed was the story of the Widow's Mite, enacted for real as glorious testimony to the providence of God!

Now, how are *you* going to respond?

Questions and Exercises

- What would happen to your neighbourhood if every member of your church sacrificed two hours per week for service in the community?
- What would happen to your *church*, if this happened?
- Why isn't this happening already? What are the obstacles that prevent it from happening?
- What can you do to remove these obstacles?
- Now, *start to remove those obstacles!*

<h1 style="text-align:center">9</h1>

Free to Work

The darkness grips the face of the land like a clammy hand. The rock front glares down like a skull at the grim scene beneath.

Here in this poor Third World country, three prisoners are being slowly and publicly tortured to death, their cries of torment attracting the attention of travellers passing through this busy crossroads. Some stop to jeer, while others pass by ashen at the abomination of it all. This is the most lingering and painful form of death ever devised; a testimony to human cruelty.

One of the prisoners, the middle one, regains some composure and, in the Aramaic tongue, cries out in his torment. 'Eloi, Eloi, lama sabachthani!' he wails as can only a man forsaken by God, with the sins of the whole world on his shoulders.

Bystanders look up and see a delirious captive crying out to the prophet Elijah; some gaze up at a sane and composed man quoting from the Psalms; one man, John, looks and sees God's only begotten son dying an atoning death in propitiation of sin. It's been this way for hours. Everyone sees whom they want to see, and imposes their own expectations upon him.

All of history and the whole unborn future meet. The most significant event ever to happen on the planet Earth is about to occur in a few minutes' time.

But wait, there's an interruption. A thief hanging alongside has turned to the central figure (in *history* as well as in this tableau) and posed a simple request, 'Lord, remember me when you come into your Kingdom.'

Does this criminal understand the *nature* of the Kingdom? Does this insignificant little man know whom he is addressing? He has already admitted that he himself is justly deserving of death, and he turns to a person whom he says has done nothing wrong, but does he really understand the *theology* of repentance? Does he understand about the forgiveness of sins? Where does he stand on baptism?

The man in the middle (between God and humanity, as well as between two thieves) has all the time in the world for a person whom society has rejected in the strongest possible terms. The fate of billions yet unborn *will just have to wait.* Theologians must hold their pens poised above their paper for a little bit longer, because here is one human tragedy that will not wait. Here's a man with an urgent need, and theological reflection takes a back seat while the matter is addressed.

This man crowned with thorns turns and speaks directly to the repentant thief, honouring him with a few seconds from a lifetime that now has precious few seconds remaining. There is, perhaps, comfort and acceptance in his voice. Though every word is physically painful to utter from his parched throat, he gives the dying criminal back his dignity and self-esteem with a promise that this insignificant person *is* important and *does* count for something. It's an act of social care as much as a matter of salvation. The thief's remaining minutes, and his eternal destiny, are transformed with a simple phrase: 'I tell you the truth. Today, you will be with me in paradise!'

Even in his dying minutes, Jesus Christ has time to give to the rejected and oppressed. World redemption has to wait upon a single 'act of change' affecting a solitary member of the community. The Man keeps the world waiting for the moment it has longed for since Adam first sinned, all for the sake of a single needy person.

The crux of history draws near. The Man pulls himself up on his bleeding wrists and prepares to speak again. Death itself is kept waiting in the wings. Is some great spiritual truth about to be spoken on his final breath? It's more important than that. He commends his weeping mother into the compassionate care of his favourite disciple. Here is a poignant pastoral moment that takes precedence over the very act of dying! Here is a good Jewish boy who looks after his mother . . .

Now, there is no more time for theology, only a moment to speak to his divine Father, whom he is now rushing to greet. Forsaken as Christ hung naked as the sin-bearer of the world, the broken Trinity itself is about to be mended! A drink of wine vinegar is offered and accepted, then the final breath of all is spent in a triumphal cry, like an athlete at the finishing line of a great race: '*It is finished.*' And I've won!

As the life passes from his body, in unseen dimensions demons laugh and every angel 'downward bends his burning eye at mysteries so bright'.

God has died, in order that we might live.

At the foot of the cross, where the author of life and architect of all creation hangs lifeless – and where the last drops of his precious blood greet the dull earth – stand three people who can only watch and wait in this darkest of hours. And that is where *we* too need to stand. Everything starts at the foot of the cross, the place of personal sacrifice. It is here that we must lay down our own lives, and work in the service of the Servant King.

Follow the Servant Son

There have been many case studies in this book that revolve around the work of people who have stood at the 'old rugged cross' and cast down their trophies for a crown. In this chapter, we look at *work* itself, the means of earning a respectable livelihood that is often denied to the poorest in society.

A church in Chapeltown, Leeds, set up a training workshop to address the needs of unemployed young people in its community. In Britain, unemployment is highest within the 16–19 age group.

Edinburgh may be Scotland's capital, and host to the world-renowned Edinburgh Festival, but it also has a serious drug problem, and a high unemployment rate (16,000 in 1996). Many of them suffer mental health problems which compound the difficulties in getting a job. 'There are 5,000 unemployed people living just one and a half miles from the church,' according to Eddie McGill, who runs the Honeycomb Project for the unemployed, from Abbeyhill Baptist Church. 'Many of our clients have no church connections, but we have seen the power of prayer making a difference to individuals' lives.'

In the United States, there is a high proportion of people who are aware of their unhelpful dependence upon welfare benefits. In contrast, in Britain, those on state benefits often seem anxious to become *more* dependent, and to receive an *increase* in benefit payments! Often, the first stage in breaking the dependence mentality is for Christians to bring home the benefits of work, in terms of the self-esteem that it bestows.

Fishy Tales!

Issaan Development Foundation (IDF) is an organisation in Northern Thailand, instigated by an American missionary who has lived there all his life. He started a project that explored *existing* missionary input in Thailand, and concluded that it was all very American – to the extent that Christianity itself was being perceived by the locals as an American faith, just as they consider Buddhism to be an Asian faith.

The missionary took a different approach and initiated two practical projects: one concerned with helping local people to develop small sustainable projects in each village (usually fish farming), and the other with church planting.

These two activities are crucially linked together, since setting up and running a village fish farm requires that people work together, pooling resources and skills through co-operation and participation. Working together invariably means that there are occasional disputes and the need to forgive each other, to 'lose face' and to be reconciled with each other. The people learned to work and live together *inter*dependently rather than in remote *in*dependence. For many Thai people this is a hard cultural lesson to learn, but changes in behaviour and attitudes become sustainable when the changes are intentionally linked to issues of an essentially spiritual nature.

When such situations are reflected upon in the context of the Christian Gospel, people's world view and their personal values change. IDF has consequently seen many Thai villagers come to Christ and many community development initiatives develop! For example, the church congregations have developed their own distinctive Thai songs and ways of communicating their faith. (This is not syncretism, but a process that gives a culturally relevant context in which worship can take place.)

Where there are fish farms operating successfully, worshipping communities are developing, because the key matter being addressed is their ability to work alongside each other, *forgiving and being reconciled one with another.*

Slavery in the UK!

It's not simply a matter of helping the unemployed to find work. The Bible is full of instructions to employers to treat their workers justly – we have come across many of them already in this book. Typical is the reference in Deuteronomy 24:14–15, to those who are casually employed on a daily basis: 'Do not take advantage of a hired man who is poor and needy . . . Pay him his wages each day before sunset, because he is poor and he is counting on it.' All civilised countries have employment laws designed to protect workers and employers alike. But there are those whom Christians should oppose, who seek to circumvent those laws.

The British Home Office gives permits to wealthy foreign families to bring into the country 'personal assistants' to help them. In theory, these permits are awarded for compassionate reasons, to allow a non-English speaker to bring in an aide on health or language grounds. Frankly, this is a racket! It's really done in order to induce these wealthy people to live – and to spend their money – in the UK. But these personal assistants are not employed under Britain's rigorous employment laws. They are regularly exploited by their employers, and are made to live in atrocious conditions.

Often they are beaten, and forced to work eighteen hours per day, with no law to protect them. They have no social security number, and no rights. Simply by granting these permits, the British government is licensing slavery! Even if a battered servant wins his or her case in court, the employers can simply leave the country to avoid having to make payment. Technically the worker is not employed in Britain, but in their home country – and paid perhaps £100 per month, when £100 per day wouldn't entice someone in Britain to do the same job.

Christians should also be outraged at sexual and racial discrimination in the workplace. Racial discrimination is twice as bad when it is combined with sexual discrimination. 'In the workplace, I perceive that women are always seen in a particular role and sometimes are not asked to aspire to anything else – they are there as a service to men,' says Bev Thomas, a black woman, adding:

Yes, sexual harassment does happen in the workplace; some women feel that they need to allow it to happen in the workplace; some women feel they just have to put up with it.

When I look at somebody who is poor, I am aware that I am often looking at somebody with low self-image, because they cannot *aspire*. I know this from my own background; I was brought up in a working-class background, and in a church where racism was an issue in the 1960s and 70s. My parents' perception was that 'this is our lot' and that, in the workplace, you just accept it.

As I grew up and sought to challenge this difference, I began saying, 'This *isn't* my lot! I am a person and I can respond!' In my own family we had three types of reaction: my parents knew it and chose to ignore it, secondly, my sisters knew it and chose to be aggressive, and finally I know it and by the grace of God seek to respond to it biblically.

A spiritual transformation is required, which will only take place if there is a Christian agenda in place – this is a fundamental difference between secular and Christian community transformation. This agenda is one which needs to be followed by all Christians, as part of their walk with God, if their own career and livelihood are not to be excluded from God's sovereignty in their lives. The agenda gives a high priority to the concepts of servanthood, leadership and vocation, in the context of transformation.

The King's Servant

'Servanthood is the biblical means of acquiring power to lead,' writes Vishal Mangalwadi in his book *Truth and Social Reform*. He sees service as an alternative power for social change, and advocates the way of the cross as the preferred Christian lifestyle.

Those who are prepared to take up the cross themselves and follow in their master's sandal prints can find that they too have a heavy price to pay, and they may even be called to make the ultimate sacrifice. Though he is now a writer and publisher, from 1976 to 1983 Vishal worked for the Association for Comprehensive Rural Assistance (ACRE). During 1982, Vishal and a dozen of his colleagues were arrested on four separate occasions, 'because we not only helped the victims of a hail-storm, but through our services exposed the insensitivity of the politicians towards the victims of this national calamity. The politicians not only had us arrested, but they also tried to have me murdered. The superintendent of police himself threatened this.'

Christians in India have been zealous for social justice since the days of William Carey. They were successful in their campaign against the unjust exploitation of indigo growers in Bengal in the nineteenth century, and their quest for social reform continued on issues as diverse as forced prostitution and bride burning. 'A society cannot be reformed until it is first informed of what is wrong with it, what is right, and how to get it right,' writes Vishal. Every Christian has a role to play in this proclamation, and in service to the hurting and the broken the world over. In God's Kingdom there are no passengers, only workers. In the world's eyes, in Christ's day, the cross was a mark of shame; it's only our consumer society that has turned it into a fashionable piece of jewellery.

People won't like you for being in God's service. They killed Jesus for the example that he set. Of the apostles, all but St John died painful deaths. Down the cascading centuries, many who called him Lord have gladly died in his service; they have fallen in love with him so deeply and deliriously, that nothing else has mattered but to be his servant.

Yes, *serve* him we must! And, through him, become servant to our own local communities. 'But I can't do that!' you plead. Yes, you can; through God's strength you can. But it's going to be tough, make no mistake.

The Servant King

That Jesus is a trouble-maker, mark my words! If he'd lived in your street when you were a kid, your mum wouldn't have let you play with him!

He's not an easy person to serve. You invite him into your house and he brings a streetful of beggars and cripples with him. He scratches your tiles with his filthy sandals; he hangs his crown of thorns in the hallway; and he props his rude wooden cross against the telly, where it drips blood all over your nice new carpet. Whatever will the neighbours think! In our churches, we've made Christ as comfy as a pair of old slippers; but he's ready to burst out like wildfire!

Christ's teaching down the centuries has been slowly modified to make it more acceptable to surrounding society. The doctrine of grace has been misused by some to cover their disobedience to God's radical principles. Christ's message is no less radical than a total inversion of the established social order. He points to a Kingdom where God's agenda is followed as sovereign decree, where the divine word is undisputed law. As Donald Kraybill writes in *The Upside-down Kingdom*: 'The Kingdom points us not to the place of God, but to the act of God. It is his ruling activity. The Kingdom is present whenever women and men submit themselves to God's reign in their lives.'

The cost of servanthood is high, but so are the rewards, in this world and the next. Jesus promised: 'Everyone who has left houses or brothers or sisters or father or mother or children or fields for my sake will receive a hundred times as much and will inherit eternal life' (Matt. 19:29). 'Where your treasure is, there your heart will be also' (Matt. 6:21). Once we become his followers, our only questions are: 'What *sort* of a servant are we going to be?' and '*Where* are we going to serve?'

We want to yield up our armies of selfish passions, and surrender ourselves to God's will, but how do we achieve that when we are sitting bleary-eyed on the top deck of a bus on our way to work at 8.20 on a Monday morning? Heaven can seem a long way away when you're stuck in a traffic jam on a dismal, rainy day. Well, perhaps you're not *meant* to be going into work on that bus. Are you *sure* you're in the right job? If it feels infeasibly hard to get enthusiastic about going to work, week after week, then you may not be in the right occupation.

There is nothing amiss in a Christian being a doctor or a truck driver. But the wise Christian doctor will refuse a posh Harley Street practice in favour of a run-down community, perhaps abroad, where the work will be truly life-saving and life-transforming. A Christian truck driver will take a local job on a lower salary, in order to remain near his wife and family, rather than a better paid job that will take him away from home for days or weeks on end. Our skills should be used to serve others, not to perpetuate inequality and self-advancement.

Ah, you say, but I never have enough money as it is; and if I change jobs, I may end up with even less. Sorry, mate; if you're working but don't have enough money, you might be spending it unwisely. Find someone in your church with a lowlier job than you, and it's a 'dead cert' that they're earning even less than you. Ask that person how he or she manages with so little money! Plead with the person to look through your outgoings with you, and to recommend ways of economising. *Be ruthless with yourself!*

Begin to question 'the way things are'. To accept that 'everything is established and unchangeable' is fatalistic. Begin to examine any obstacles that prevent you from applying biblical ethics to your own situations, and prayerfully to explore God's plan for your career. Ask God to show you his plan for your life. Explore the Scriptures and consider the following ways in which God might also work to give you his guidance:

God's will for us is written into the fibre of our being, as he calls us through our *gifting* – the things that we are good at! Our talents largely determine our occupation – if you're in a job because it pays better than the one that makes best use of your talents, then you're probably in the wrong job! It might be that you are already in the right career, but that you are intended to be performing some voluntary work, too; or the Lord might be asking you to change jobs. We need to work alongside people who feel a similar call, while deferring to those who are more experienced or better trained than ourselves. God also calls us through the urgent needs of others, though often we are oblivious to these needs. Like Peter, James and John, we are sleeping in Gethsemane. We have to awaken to a dirty, cruel world whose people are shrieking with pain, crying out for the cup of suffering to pass from them.

Sometimes, people don't realise that it's *part of their current job* to hear and respond to those calls, and it takes an unexpected event to bring it to our attention. A group of pastors found that out in a remarkable way in India.

Condemned?

Tear Fund facilitated a training workshop with its Indian partners in AIDS work that it has supported for several years. These partners

– the project leaders employed on various schemes – were told that they could come *only if they brought their pastor with them*. The church nationally was in denial of the AIDS problem at that time. But twenty-five project managers turned up, with their pastors, for a two-day workshop. In the discussions and seminars, the pastors were challenged to devise ways in which their churches could make the AIDS projects function 'better'. One pastor explained that his church had forbidden him from addressing the AIDS problem in his preaching; some pastors were enthusiastic about the work, and others less so. At the end of the conference, there was an acknow-ledgment by most pastors that the work was important, but little sense of personal commitment to the work from some of them.

After the conference, several of the more reluctant pastors were taken off to Pune, where they were led on a visit to a brothel! They sat in the hallway of this whorehouse, where fifty girls were working on beds separated only by flimsy net curtains. The children of the prostitutes ran around the room, or sat on the edge of the beds while their mother had sex with a stranger, just a couple of feet away.

In that scandalous situation, the pastors were led by a Tear Fund worker in a Bible study, on John 8:1–11, where Jesus refuses to condemn the woman caught in adultery, but requires her to make changes in her life: specifically, to 'sin no more'. The pastors were asked, 'What is the Church's role in helping a woman to change from a life of prostitution?' and they were obliged to perform their hermeneutics on the Bible passage sitting in the hallway of this Indian vice-den – its sights, sounds and smells groaning all about them.

The pastors realised that, until their churches were able to create a sense of community and a feeling of belonging, a sense of family stronger than that which the prostitute was being asked to leave, their theology would be impotent. The girls lying around them lived and worked in these cramped conditions, and it was the only community that they knew, the only life they could ever envisage leading. This was not a place for bland platitudes or pious preaching, nor for solving problems by handing out tracts.

The pastors realised that they couldn't condemn these girls, many of whom were HIV positive, because they were not able to offer these people a viable *alternative* to the lives they were leading. They were more 'sinned against' than sinning. The pastors came away chatting excitedly about their desire to address the health needs of these girls; to try to help their children; to offer the prostitutes a viable alternative lifestyle; and to provide a sense of community that is life-giving, and which gladly accepts these people who have been left with no alternative means of economic survival but to sell the only thing they have remaining to them – their own bodies.

If Christians can't immediately find a viable economic alternative, it doesn't take much to provide a mums-and-toddlers club or a creche. There are three or four days a month when a prostitute can't work anyway, and that gives a brief time in which a female church member can spend time with her and begin to assess the scale of the problem and sound out possible alternative employment. *If the Church doesn't respond to this problem, who will?*

Dry Bones, Dancing

You may think that the proposals above are hopeless, but God showed Ezekiel that he could even restore flesh to dead bones, for his glory. Several Christian groups are *already* working with prostitutes, to try to restore their self-respect, and to put them back in touch with their emotions that have been suppressed for so long. City Gates, a group from Ichthus, worked in one of London's most notorious red light districts amongst the girls and their maids, opening up a whole new world that few British Christians know anything about.

'Every prostitute has a maid, who helps to answer the door, vet the customers and – if the girl is busy with a client – asks any new callers to come back later,' explains Russell Grubb, who led the work. 'She also helps to clean, and acts as moral support. Some clients get sexually frustrated if they are unable to "perform" and can become violent.' The City Gates team prayed with the girls, and sought to share Christ with them. Unless trust and rapport could be built up, the girls would not change their lifestyles. The team were aware that many of them knew no other means of earning a living. There are no glib answers.

Making initial contact with the girls necessitated crossing what Russell felt to be a *fear* barrier. On his first trip, he took along a female member of City Gates. As they climbed a flight of stairs, a pimp opened a door behind them blocking their retreat, and stood glaring at them:

'We felt a tremendous wall of fear. We either had to back off or stand our ground. In the end, the pimp backed off from us, returned to his room and closed the door. We knocked on the prostitute's door and *gave her flowers*.' This display of regard and respect, after being used as little more than a piece of meat all day long, was the crucial breakthrough. There have been successes. Several girls have become Christians and left the area. Other girls who sold sex only occasionally have come to Christ, but have remained prostitutes – often to support heroin addiction. Total transformation to a 'normal' Christian lifestyle is often a costly business, which can be achieved only with time. *Is it a type of work that **your church** could take on?*

It's not only former prostitutes that can have a difficult time adjusting to the Christian faith, and finding respectable regular employment. The same applies to former *witches* who, when they abandon their previous lifestyle, find that they miss the closeness of relationships they have known within a coven. A Bible study group or home group often constitutes a poor replacement for the intensity of person interaction to which they have become accustomed.

'I came from a large family – I have sixteen brothers and one sister. Father was a tremendously romantic human being!' laughs the Puerto Rican, before describing a home background that could have come straight out of a horror movie. 'Father was a Satanic priest and mother was a witch. The combination of darkness was destroying not only myself, but also my brothers and sister. The Bible was totally forbidden, and no one said a prayer to Jesus Christ.

Animals were sacrificed and all manner of secret things took place.' When this man moved to New York, before he was scarcely out of his childhood, orgies and debasement became part of his way of life. 'I was like a zombie. I watched my best friend die – after I had taught him how to cheat and kill. I realised that there was one thing I had forgotten – I hadn't taught him how to die.'

How can a church reach a person like this? It took a very special preacher, named David Wilkerson, with a very special ministry, named Teen Challenge, to relate to this young man in his own terms and to give him back a sense of dignity and self-worth. Only then could David bring him to God, by showing trust – asking this untrustworthy young man to take the collection at a Gospel rally! So began the transformation from New York gang leader to international evangelist. This Puerto Rican male is, of course, Nicky Cruz.

Nicky now feels that there ought to be an excitement in our churches to counter the attractions offered by witchcraft: 'But we have become so caught up in theology that we forget there is a lot of pain, rejection and fear in life. I don't believe the Church is really responding to that.'

Treasures out of Darkness

Sonny Arguinzoni began snorting heroin at the age of thirteen. Completely unemployable, he ran with the gang from his asphalt jungle neighbourhood when they fought a rival gang from the lower east side of Manhattan, and graduated to 'mainlining' on heroin – injecting the drug, for the greater 'rush' it gave.

Sonny began stealing cars and joyriding before selling the vehicles to a backstreet 'fence' to support his addiction. On one such joyride, his friends Frankie and Duke were killed when their stolen Cadillac crashed. He was jailed for six months. Living on the cutting edge, Sonny started housebreaking. His gang soon controlled most of the drugs in his neighbourhood. Then a skinny preacher turned up on the block and announced himself as David Wilkerson . . . But wait! Sonny came to Christ, brought not by David, but through the ministry of Nicky Cruz!

Sonny married Julie, who had seen her own brother overdose on heroin, and together they began to minister to prostitutes, drug addicts and those whom society rejects as the dregs.   >>*Fast forward three decades and switch location to Holloway, North London, in August 1994>>*   Sonny, now with a little less hair and broader of girth, and the head of Victory Outreach International, is standing on the platform of a tent crusade, preaching up a storm. His thousand-strong audience is unlike any that you've ever seen at a tent crusade before. Here is a multi-racial group of young people who wouldn't be seen dead in a church; indeed, their tattoos, pierced body parts, filthy jeans and wild hairstyles would give most Christians a fright! Glazed eyes and dilated pupils from drug abuse are common, but these needy people hear the Gospel message loud and clear.

Attractive posters for *Young Gangstas* had been flyposted all over London, presenting the four-night run in an appealing way which related well to young Londoners. It was an amateur production about street gangs, but every cast member had personally lived that lifestyle, and presented the play in a far more authentic manner than any professional cast could have achieved. In seventy minutes or so, there were depictions of crime, violence, intravenous heroin addiction, marijuana smoking and whisky drinking. Characters spoke of sexual abuse at the hands of their parents, and of selling their bodies on the street to support their drug addictions. Rap and dance music played constantly in the background. The shootings were very realistic, and the fate of the 'bad guy' – stabbed with a pair of scissors in a prison barber's shop – was suitably messy. But beneath the blood and gore, real human emotions were enacted. Seconds after the 'hero' made his commitment to Christ, in a prison visiting room, Sonny walked on stage and gave an altar call lasting all of thirty seconds. It was the only 'sermon' of the evening. The drama and music had carried the Gospel with little need for spoken commentary.

Young Gangstas won many for Christ that evening, transforming their lives by being culturally relevant to the streetlife of the young people at whom it was aimed. They identified with the characters in the play, and could confront their own failings through them. *Christ was glorified in the very heart of darkness.* In Los Angeles, Victory Outreach International has attracted up to 14,000 gang members to single performances. *Now, THAT's reaching unreachable people for Christ.*

In an office in the nearby women's home, where prostitutes and addicts are rehabilitated as part of Pastor Sonny's global ministry to the destitute – *and that is how to transform your converts* – Sonny Arguinzoni chats as Art Blajas, former hitman for the Mexican Mafia, pours coffee. Sonny is now in overall charge of two hundred growing churches, and two hundred rehabilitation centres, in countries through north, central and south America, and Europe, but he remains modest and unassuming:

> It's been a slow start, but we now have this building that attracts drug addicts and prostitutes, and people are experiencing deliverance. We disciple these people who become future evangelists. There is a whole revolution that God is performing within the inner city. There is a sub-culture of people that don't fit easily into a church, and who need to be re-trained if they are ever to be employable.

Quite. There's not a lot of demand for assassins in God's kingdom!
Is this a type of work with which **you** *could be involved, either full-time or as a part-time volunteer?*

Your Personal Golgotha

Church leader Adrian Hawkes pushed his own church into the community, by making good use of various government employment programmes that ran through most of the seventies and eighties.

> We employed people on those schemes, using them mainly for building work that was of use to the community. I saw it restore

confidence in people, who then went out and got themselves permanent jobs. Working in partnership with a group in the Wirral, we employed around 700 people at one time. I employed several disabled people – using one to translate government gobbledy-gook into real English! – and the work experience set them up to gain other employment.

In the 1990s, Adrian and his wife started fostering children:

There is a desperate need for foster parents in the UK. I got into it myself almost by accident, but when I saw the need and realised that Christians could do something about it, I talked about it in my church and we now have at least ten fosterers in the congregation, nearly 10 per cent of all the fosterers in Haringey! We enjoy working with the local authority, and they seem to enjoy working in partnership with us. It's small, but it solves a big problem at the end.

My theory is that, if a church and community are willing to work together, there's nothing they can't achieve. If people are only going to look after themselves, 'doing their own thing', there isn't much hope. Take the story of the Tower of Babel. The people building the tower had a common language, so communication was good; there was a common goal, so they all agreed what was to be done; and there was a common will to work. None of this was for a godly purpose, but God said about these people, 'Nothing they plan to do will be impossible for them' (Gen. 11:6). Where there is a real desire by Christians to work in the community, nothing can stop them. I've found this true in several church situations that I oversee.

Churches and individual Christians alike must be willing to:

- Forsake some of their individualism to pursue a common goal.
- Attempt communication – which isn't always easy.
- Work together to achieve something.

Work bestows dignity on the worker, whether or not he or she is paid for the labour. Some people take on voluntary work in addition to their paid work; others, perhaps married to a breadwinner, find it a more just use of their free time than working for personal gain; while others do it to gain experience while unemployed. Some of the reasons why people become volunteers on community projects are well considered and tightly defined, while others can be extremely vague. Here are some reasons that were put forward by volunteers from one particular project:

- 'I got involved because it was there.'
- 'I drifted in gradually. I believe I'm giving a service to people who need it.'
- 'I believe in practical Christianity.'
- 'If I say I love God, I should also love my fellow men and women.'
- 'It's very much part of the Christian message.'
- 'It's living out a responsibility in a way I know is helpful.'

'If everybody does a little bit, the job gets done, even if it's a massive undertaking,' says Adrian. 'It's amazing how little effort is required to achieve so much, but it requires people to see that working together is better than working individually; and for people to see that their own small contribution is part of the bigger picture, and helps the jigsaw to come together.'

Helping to transform their communities is something that Christians in the West can actually do that is practical, at a local level. It enables us to 'think globally but act locally', using strategies that have been tried and tested across the globe. Here are some more ideas of ways you could help, as an individual or as a church.

CARE Leyton

We met David Ainge, and his work with Faith in Action, in chapter six. Closer to home, David is also involved with a local church-sponsored 'good neighbour' scheme, working alongside nine other local churches across the major denominations. The aim is to meet emergency needs from anyone in the local community. In its first three years, the scheme has received around 1,000 calls for help.

Some of the needs have been very simple and basic: taking a prescription to the chemist, transporting a person to a clinic, befriending an old person, or shopping for a house-bound person. Basic do-it-yourself – mending fuses, changing light bulbs or fixing a plug – is also provided. If someone is depressed because the long grass outside their window is restricting their view, then that too will be handled by a volunteer.

'The basic rule of thumb is, if you would do it for your next-door neighbour, then we offer it to our community,' David explains:

We have *one* telephone number which people can ring to ask for help. These calls are re-routed daily from the BT box inside my entrance porch to the dozen or so duty helpers. These people assess the emergency need and match the suitability of various volunteers to address the problem. The CARE Leyton 'office' is contained in a humble suitcase, with all the documents needed to run the scheme. It travels from house to house each day, so there is an enormous saving in office rental. Our major cost is the expense of having BT re-direct the call. We have over a hundred volunteers, who each have the right to decline a task if it is too inconvenient; this takes the pressure off volunteers. Being people of goodwill, they respond readily and frequently.

As an extension of the scheme, those local people who would have been alone on Christmas Day have been invited to a meal, free of charge. This Christ-centred service transformed the festive season for those Christians involved.

There are three basic kinds of task:

- The light, person-centred type: washing someone's hair, cooking a meal, doing some shopping.
- Property-based jobs: the do-it-yourself tasks outlined earlier.

- Transport tasks: taking someone to a hospital, shop, or even hairdresser.

The agenda is set by the client, and matched to the range of volunteers available at that particular time. It's rare for CARE Leyton ever to say 'No', unless the request is beyond the competence one could expect of a lay volunteer. Another exception might be if there is a relative nearby who could easily do the job, when there might be another person in need who has no relatives in the world.

Many practical problems had to be overcome before the scheme could commence. The task was too big for any one church to resource, so several neighbouring churches had to be 'sold' on the idea; here local organisations like the Council of Churches were helpful in networking different congregations. Then a complex administrative system had to be thrashed out, to ensure the logging of calls and assignment of volunteers; these volunteers had to be recruited and trained, after references had been taken up. Each founder church provided £100 in start-up funding, which covered the cost of producing advertising and literature. Even in the impoverished East End of London, income has exceeded expenditure each year.

Is this the kind of ministry which **your** *church could try?*

Over to You

If *you* want to do something significant in *your* community, the first step is to find someone who wants to do it with you! If you can't relate strongly to one Christian person and to share the vision, then how are you going to live out the vision in a community where believers are in a minority? Christians and people of goodwill, working together, make a potent team. And, through the 'working together' they may catch the opportunity to reflect on Gospel values. *That's the 'bottom line'.*

The Church needs working ministries that meet not only today's needs, but tomorrow's challenges as well; that carry through the vision that God has given to individuals, and allow it to flow into a shared community life; that involve lay involvement in positions of responsibility; and that are self-reliant and cross-denominational, sowing the seeds of freedom, justice and mercy.

Questions and Exercises

- What are the obstacles that prevent *you* from applying biblical principles to your own personal situation?
- Pick two aspects of the schemes described in this chapter that you think might be applicable in your own local community.
- What special difficulties would you expect to encounter in starting such specific ministries in your own neighbourhood?
- Share the vision with your Christian friends, and find at least two others who will prayerfully share the vision with you.
- Gain some experience by undertaking some part-time voluntary work with someone else's scheme in your area.

10

Free to Live

Sarah de Carvalho had the world at her feet.

Her glittering career in TV production and film promotion had taken her to far-flung corners of the globe. By 1990, she was earning £1,000 per week working as a producer at Sky Television, but God had other plans for her life: 'I want you to go to Brazil.' The next year found her, a life of affluence abdicated, working with street children on the dusty streets of Belo Horizonte. A diary entry, from her book *The Street Children of Brazil*, reads:

April 5th 1991. O Lord, I was so shocked to see the children and where they live under the freeways in cardboard boxes. The gang we visited were so high on glue and 'tiner' (stronger than paint thinner) that they couldn't walk or speak properly. The whole place stank of urine and faeces. There were about eleven of them in all, only three were girls. The youngest was nine years old and the eldest, the leader, was seventeen. But most of the teenagers looked ten years old through bad nutrition.

Most of the girls in these gangs were pregnant by the time they were twelve. AIDS was rife.

At the time, Brazil had a domestic deficit of $25,000,000,000 and a $115,000,000,000 foreign debt, which left 70 per cent of its 150,000,000 people on or below the poverty line. These destitute children were the casualties of the West's economic greed.

Sarah's inspirational story is one of transformed lives. After working with YWAM in Rio de Janeiro, she and her husband set up the Happy Child Mission, on a farm where street children could be taken out of their city environment and allowed to rediscover their childhood. Many have discovered Christ for themselves as a result of the practical concern that has been shown for them by Sarah and other Christians. *But there is so much more to be done.* Worldwide, an estimated 100,000,000 homeless 'street children' struggle for survival.

Invitation to Care

It is difficult to get on with your life if you have no roof over your head. We talk of homeless people having 'nowhere to *live*', for it seems as though life itself grinds to a halt when you have no accommodation. Without a home, there is only the drudgery of *existence*, with nowhere private to keep your belongings, to invite friends, to conduct a relationship, to have a family, or simply to be alone. Without a home, it's virtually impossible to hold down a job; a potential employer will want to know 'where do you live' and without an address there'll be no job offer. That's not living, it's merely surviving.

Mike Fearon ran several community projects in Huddersfield, West Yorkshire, in the 1970s, including a soup run. It wasn't difficult, though it was very time-consuming. In the 1980s, he helped to establish a hostel in Hackney, east London, for homeless young people – it took four years of gestation before taking in the first residents. In the 1990s, he helped to develop and lead an innovative resettlement project in Newham, which took four years to reach the point where it could employ its first full-time staff member. The lesson is clear: *patience and tenacity are essential to make any headway in this kind of work.* It's an enormous task. No fewer than 125,640 households were accepted as homeless by councils in England alone in 1995.

The satisfaction of seeing someone finally come off the streets makes it all worthwhile. While working with refugees in 1996, Mike managed to resettle several asylum seekers in accommodation of their own. He vividly remembers one African woman, who spoke only French, and who had spent several weeks sleeping in nightshelters and staying with various friends. She looked about forty, with a heavy-set face. When Mike found her a humble bed-sitter which several homeless people from the UK had previously turned down, her whole face lit up. She looked quite ecstatic and the whole shape of her face changed. She produced a warm and contagious smile, and suddenly appeared fifteen years younger!

A Dose of TLC

Barry Lock, Chief Executive of the Christian charity OASIS Trust, first worked with the Trust's International Director, Steve Chalke, back in the days when Steve was Assistant Minister and Barry a church-based social worker, in Tonbridge, Kent. Barry remembers that their first project, setting up a hostel in Southwark, south London, was initially resisted by the local authority: '"Over our dead bodies!" was their attitude.' Several years later, the local authority has come to support and acclaim the work, which seeks to be the best in its field.

People perceive a need to help homeless young people, but often misinterpret it, thinking that homelessness can be solved just through soup runs, when the *long-term solution* is to come up with accommodation and support – as well as tackling basic causes. 'It's the evangelical disease – to go for the quick answer. With evangelism, too, we always look for short cuts instead of investing time with the people we want to see come to Christ,' says Steve. 'As well as hostels, we need to give people on the streets the care, education and counselling that they need.'

David Evans commenced work with Oasis in 1990 to develop strategies for healthcare for homeless people – with the aim of reconnecting the homeless with mainstream healthcare, rather than to create a separate system for them. 'Lizzies', a primary healthcare centre for the homeless, now attracts some 8,000 homeless people each year.

Nursing services are provided, together with basic hygiene facilities, a clothing exchange and a laundry. The clients enjoy using the centre, because they are made to feel very welcome and very special. Never a week goes by without someone new turning up at the door, because the 'word on the street' amongst the homeless is that Lizzies is a cut above many other projects.

The project works in partnership with the local health authority, and it has forged an excellent relationship with the local GP practice. It is funded largely by the London Borough Grants Unit, but some £60,000 per year has to be raised from outside sources. The Nurse Manager and her deputy are both qualified nurses, but the rest of the staff come without formal training. This is not a job which requires medical expertise, but rather a great love for people. Here, the medicine most frequently given is a large spoonful of TLC. Tender Loving Care soothes the cares of those forsaken by society, and heals broken hearts more effectively than any prescribed drug.

Yeast!

The work of Oasis Trust embraces training and evangelism as well as social action. By 1997, Oasis employed four full-time evangelists, operating in both traditional and more modern ways. A travelling evangelistic presentation was intended to appeal to young people, through a striking contemporary format. Increasingly, there are connections between the evangelistic initiatives and social action.

Relationships are the key to good evangelism, and relationships are often best formed through social care. Barry Lock argues:

> There are some very arbitrary distinctions drawn between social action and evangelism. Personal salvation is part and parcel of the Gospel, but the Gospel is often perceived in such a narrow way. We've seen people come to Christ through the social welfare programme, often through Oasis street teams, comprising volunteers who go out most nights of the week. People are responsive, though the Gospel is not pushed down people's throats. Different teams have different emphases, some are more openly evangelistic than others, but that's okay. There are other volunteers who are far more confident just giving out sandwiches.
>
> We have a bus that goes out with the street teams. The users themselves have asked for a Bible study, so we've organised one on the top deck on one of the nights. Good practice is about being responsive to people's needs.

When Christians begin to spread themselves through different aspects of a person's life – the physical as well as the spiritual; the emotional as well as the intellectual – then their witness to the Gospel, and the values it represents, can begin to act as a yeast. Personal growth becomes possible in a holistic manner, as all aspects of a person's life begin to change and develop together.

Hear the Heartbeat

Though born in Britain, Dave Andrews has lived most of his life in Australia. He is a deep thinker, who has a rare gift of interpreting the activities and motivations of any society in which he finds himself, and contrasting it with the biblical ideal. He speaks carefully, seeking constant assurance that he is being correctly understood – something we would all do well to emulate!

With that gift, it was natural that he would find himself in a pulpit before he was out of his teens. Fortunately, his father was a

Baptist minister, and able to offer his son the possibility of preaching engagements. Dave Andrews, though, had no illusions about the Church: 'I used to struggle with what I felt was a total misrepresentation of Christ!' he laughs. 'No matter how many evangelistic programmes our church sponsored, the way our church related to the community was basically de-evangelistic; it didn't give people a reason to believe in God, but rather gave them a reason to curse God.'

When he began to preach, at the age of fifteen, he used to confront churches with those things – and call for a profound change. Doubtless some congregations regarded him, at that stage, as an upstart – particularly when he took to visiting churches the week before he was due to preach, dressing like a homeless person in ragged clothes, to take notes on how people treated him.

'Then I'd turn up the next week in my glad rags to confront them!' he says, practically rolling on the floor with laughter. 'Needless to say, though I used to get a lot of invitations to preach, I never got invited back!' It sounds a bit like Christ, who – we read in Scripture – used to be invited to dine with the rich, but we never read about him being invited back . . .

Tea in the Slums

In 1975, Dave and his wife found themselves in India working largely with foreign travellers who had gone there in search of 'enlightenment' during the drug-crazed hippie era. From there, he began to work in the slums and resettlement areas, addressing some of the social, political and economic issues that India presents. As they worked amongst drug-dependents, the suicidal and the oppressed of Delhi, several worshipping communities eventually developed:

> We don't immediately present ourselves as Christians. Like Jesus, we work alongside people and develop credibility. Over a period of time, people discovered that Jesus was the Christ; similarly,

we work with people on the basis of common sense – believing that, because people are made in the image of God, something of God's will for them reveals itself in their own consciousness, whether they recognise it or not. For example, the police used to be aggressive and the people we worked with used to respond by throwing rocks at the police station – which only made them more aggressive! So we sat down and asked if there was a better way of dealing with the situation. People suggested inviting the police over for a cup of tea, and it worked really well!

Having established that the approach worked, we pointed out to the local people that it was consistent with what Jesus used to say about blessing those that curse you. Basically, we affirmed a way of dealing with things; got them to work on it; and, once they had done it, we would make *explicit* the *implicit* connections in the decisions. We did that over and over again, until they began to develop a respect and regard for Jesus, because it seemed that what he said was good and right was in line with what they had proved to be workable. Eventually, the time came when the people, before they made a decision, habitually came to ask, 'I wonder what Jesus would do in this situation?' Then we could find a Gospel principle which related to the situation. If they took that principle as their framework, then the process of conversion had begun.

On one occasion, bulldozers moved in ready to demolish the dwellings in which the community lived, and the people asked Dave what Jesus would have done in the same situation: 'One of the guys remembered the story that Jesus told about a little old lady who, because of her persistence, got the authorities to do what they should have done in the first place. The people were inspired by the biblical story and organised petitions and marches to save their homes.' They got a staying order to halt the bulldozers, then they were given land and resources to rebuild their community. Not everybody remembered that everything had worked out well because they had followed the biblical pattern, but some people did and they joined the worshipping Christian community in the slums of Delhi.

Table in the Desert

In spite of the good work which Dave did amongst the poor, he was eventually thrown out by the Indian government. 'I cried for six months,' he says. 'I felt I was finished.' But back in Australia, he found that the principles that he had laboriously worked out over the years in India applied equally well amongst trade union groups in Queensland: 'There has been a lot of conflict in our state between unions and government. Our premier made Margaret Thatcher look like a liberal!' Unfortunately, he was also a Lutheran Christian who must have made Christ seem, to unbelievers, like Attila the Hun . . .

Often the trade unions called strikes to press their case, but in so doing they alienated the public. Dave spoke to the state trade union leaders and advocated that, when they went on strike, all their members should go and do voluntary work in the community. That way, they not only confronted the government, they also persuaded the public that the unionists were the good guys.

I'm part of a network in our area called 'The Waiters Group'. We wait on God, and on our neighbours. We don't set the agendas, we just hang around and do what we can to help. We're trying to give contemporary expression to the notion of a servant church, in our locality. We encourage everyone in the church to get involved with their neighbours, and disadvantaged groups in the area, spending as much time as possible with them, to discover what the needs are, and how they can come alongside those people and help with their needs.

Activism comes from interaction. We try to live a life of quiet help and loud protests.

One piece of strident protest – 'to give a voice to those who cannot speak for themselves' – involved *giving away money in a local shopping precinct.* When Dave felt that candidates in a local election were 'buying' votes by competing to promise the biggest tax reductions, instead of addressing serious social problems such as homelessness:

We wanted to demonstrate that, while our society is preoccupied with greed, issues of justice will never become crucial or rate a significant mention on political agendas. Giving money away demonstrated both the greed itself and the detachment from it of the Waiters Group. A lot of commentators said that people would have too much dignity to fight over the two-dollar bills (worth about £1 in UK currency) that we were handing out. But when the day came, there were crowds of people fighting, kicking and stamping to get the money off us. It was just a riot! *It was a telling parable of the forces at work in our society . . .*

When the local community was feeling oppressed by exploitive landlords, and anarchist groups were talking about 'shoving chain-saws up the bums of landlords', the Waiters Group became catalysts. Dave went on a hunger strike to protest against the greed that was destroying the community. In addition to exposing greedy landlords, the group was careful also to commend those landlords that were adopting a responsible attitude – by giving them flowers in the main street, with television cameras in attendance!

Dave organised a protest to expose ruthless landlords by sleeping outside their houses. This destroyed their anonymity, and demon-strated the homelessness that they were causing. This, again, was covered by prime-time television. The police were supportive of this protest, which unmasked the abuse of market forces. The Waiters Group were more effective than the local unionists, because the spiritual dimension they represented was more holistic and mean-ingful than the trade unionists' mere ideologies.

Peacock's Tale

Chris Peacock was born in the West Indies, to Christian parents who saw around them great poverty. It never occurred to his family to distinguish between preaching the Gospel and looking after people. 'They started Jamaica's first building society, run by Christians, and other businesses that employed people, but they never saw it as social action. They just felt this was something that Christians have to do. If they didn't look after people, who would?' Chris moved to London and began working in advertising, eventually working his way up to a directorship, before leaving to set up his own company. He currently works in a senior management post at Scripture Union.

'After I stopped working in advertising, I decided to write a novel about a homeless person!' says Chris, who also heads up the voluntary work of the All Souls Local Action Network (ASLAN) based at All Souls, Langham Place, in central London. 'It never came to anything, but, after I joined All Souls Church, I heard an appeal for volunteers to help with the work amongst the homeless. I put two and two together and wondered if the connection was God's way of getting me involved.'

ASLAN had begun in 1988, and stemmed from a weekend away undertaken by the church's 20/20 group – logically enough, for people in their twenties. A call that several people had felt through Bible study over the course of the weekend was reinforced by a sermon preached by John Stott on the Sunday evening. Soon, a tea run had been set up, going out to various central London locations where homeless people tended to congregate, in the early hours of Saturday morning. Five teams operated a rota system, which soon attracted around a hundred volunteers, from All Souls and other churches.

'When I signed up for the tea run, I was told that they already had enough volunteers,' Chris remembers. 'So I was invited to join a new work. ASLAN had just begun at The Passage day centre in Victoria, which needed five more teams on a rota, to operate from 9.00 a.m. to midday every Saturday.'

Baptism of Fire!

Chris Peacock continues:

It was a shock to discover that one of the tasks that the volunteers were expected to do was to clean up after each morning's session

– and that extended to cleaning the toilets! The team leader at the time had a rule that the last team member to arrive had to clean the loos at the end of the morning; since I was always the last, I was consistently the one with the rubber gloves on! I remember saying to God, 'If I'd known that I was going to turn into the bog washer when I volunteered to do this, I doubt that I would have agreed!' It was an *interesting* experience . . .

Meeting with the homeless people for the first time, I was conscious that I didn't know what to do or say. I was frightened that I might say the wrong thing. I had all kinds of preconceptions of what homeless people were like. A number of clients that I met that first day mumbled incomprehensibly, and I didn't know whether to say 'No', 'Yes', 'Pardon', or if I should just mumble back. It was a real baptism of fire.

When I took over the leadership of ASLAN a few years later, one of the first things I did was to prepare a fact sheet of 'do's' and 'don'ts' to send out to new volunteers. I wanted them to be guided a little more than *I* had been, though new volunteers still come with preconceptions. They often expect the homeless to be a homogenous group of people, and they are quite surprised when they find that they are as diverse as any normal bunch of people you could expect to find. They are chalk and cheese: some are charming and well-educated, others have no education at all; some are drunk and aggressive, others are timid and quiet; many are hurt and angry. When I'm asked, 'Can you give us a guide on how to deal with homeless people?' I tell them, 'Sorry, I can't. They are so varied in background and current circumstances.'

Some volunteers worry about the possible personal risk to themselves, but it's much lower than people think. 'I've seen homeless people put up with behaviour by other homeless people which, if it happened in an ordinary West End pub, would instantly lead to a knife fight!' says Chris. 'Many homeless people, because of the rage, pain and hurt inside them, can be quite verbally abusive. I've seen remarkably few examples of physical abuse, and no major injury.'

There is a minute tuberculosis risk, but volunteers can get a test done if they are worried they may have contracted something nasty. There is a minute risk of AIDS infection, but if proper precautions are taken – never coming into contact with body fluids without wearing rubber gloves – there is nothing to cause alarm. If you focus on being a servant rather than a leader, and a listener rather than a talker, you'll do fine in this sort of voluntary work.

ASLAN has experienced far fewer awkward moments with its clients than it has with other Christians . . .

Pass the Salt

The Church long since has moved on from the days of George Orwell, when homeless people were seen as Gospel fodder, denied food until they'd sat through a fire and brimstone sermon. But still, some critics demand aggressively to know why ASLAN doesn't preach the Gospel at its clients; after all, it has a captive audience. Chris replies:

> We *show* the Gospel, and I *invite* people to a place where the Gospel is preached, namely my own church and other churches. I do not believe, if you look at Jesus' ministry, that he always preached in every situation; and, unlike us, he came *specifically* to proclaim the good news of God making peace with mankind. In spite of that definite ministry, he never once turned to anyone who asked to be healed and said, 'Repent of your sins and *then* I will heal you.' On every single occasion, he healed the person's physical ailment before addressing the spiritual needs.

The core of the Gospel is that Jesus Christ, in whom dwells the fullness of the Godhead, lived on earth as a person – fully human and fully divine – and died a sacrificial death in order that our sins might be forgiven, after repentance, by grace, through faith in Christ's atonement. But there is no evidence in the Gospels that Jesus preached this himself! In his earthly ministry, the Lord never referred publicly to his own divinity, and he only hinted obliquely at his own imminent death. In public, he seems (from Mark 4:34) to have spoken in parables and very largely to have *allowed his actions to speak for themselves.* He explained himself more fully to his disciples, but only in private. For the apostles, preaching the Gospel *in isolation from the works and lifestyle which support it* was simply not a normal biblical pattern.

In the Nazareth synagogue at the commencement of his mission, Christ announced a Messianic agenda that some would say amounted to a creed for social action. Quoting from Isaiah, he read: 'The Spirit of the Lord is on me, because he has anointed me to preach good news to the poor. He has sent me to proclaim freedom for the prisoners and recovery of sight for the blind, to release the oppressed, to proclaim the year of the Lord's favour' (Luke 4:18, 19). *Hey Jesus! You missed out the spiritual bit about saving souls!*

Of course, for Christ, there was no separation between a person's spiritual, emotional, mental and physical needs – the very idea is totally alien to his theology! In his manifesto of God's Kingdom – the Sermon on the Mount – he described the lifestyle he expected from his followers, but didn't say much about the cross, or his own atoning blood. The practical implication and outworking of the Kingdom were more than adequate to draw people to his cause, and the spiritual side would come later, at the proper time. He had dire warnings for anyone who didn't put their faith into active service:

> Not everyone who says to me, 'Lord, Lord,' will enter the kingdom of heaven, but only those who will do the will of my Father who is in heaven. Many will say to me on that day, 'Lord, Lord, did we not prophesy in your name, and in your name drive out demons and perform many miracles?' Then I will tell them plainly, 'I never knew you. Away from me, you evildoers!' (Matt. 7:21–3)

Signs and wonders, prophecy and deliverance – *faith as big as a mustard tree* – these things are all very well, but if they're all you've got, you're a couple of billiard balls short of a set!

It doesn't do to be complacent: 'You are the salt of the earth. But if the salt loses its saltiness, how can it be made salty again? It is no longer good for anything, except to be thrown out and trampled under foot' (Matt. 5:13). In Christ's day, long before refrigeration, salt was used as a preservative – to prevent meat from going bad. Christians are called to be active in society, in their culture and in their local neighbourhood, to prevent the community from becoming putrid. Anyone who doesn't want to do God's will – whose heart is not set on following the Kingdom manifesto and keeping our society fresh and hearty – is asking for trouble . . .

(Check out Matt. 24:45–51; Mark 9:43-9, 11:20-6; Luke 3:7-9, 12:35–48, 13:6–9, 14:16–35, 16:19–25, 19:11–27; John 15:5, 6; Rev 20:12, 13)

'Heretical Tendencies'?

Steve Chalke has always known that, when Jesus told him to tell people the Gospel, it involved more than just standing on a soapbox preaching: it has to meet people's real needs. He began to be fascinated by controversial aspects of the New Testament, like Jesus speaking of the sheep and goats in Matthew 25. With infectious enthusiasm, he says:

I 'knew' what evangelism was because I'd been told by the evangelical church that if people pray a prayer for forgiveness and accept Christ as their Saviour, they'll go to heaven; and if they don't, they won't. My theory is, that if anyone else but Jesus had preached that sermon in Matthew 25 they'd be slung out of the church! Even if Billy Graham had preached it, people would have said he'd developed heretical tendencies; but here Jesus says that when he judges people at the end of the world and divides the sheep from the goats, he will judge them not on the basis of what they believe, but on the basis of what they have done.

I think we've cheapened the business of being 'born again'. It should be a radical turning around and, as James points out, faith without works is dead. Jesus isn't being inconsistent with what he says in John 3:16. In Matthew 25 he is simply saying that the result of being born again is that you will feed the hungry, give drink to the thirsty and visit the prisoners, and if you don't you were never 'born again' in the first place, chum.

You may have got your doctrine off pat, and be an evangelical to your dying day, but if you didn't do anything, you've missed the boat! You totally misunderstood what being a Christian was all about. I think the evangelical church has made a huge error in getting people to become Christians, then telling them that if they want to be really, really committed, they can go to house groups or tithe. It's so banal, and so far from what Jesus was on about. *Intellectual assent is not saving faith; it's not the stuff that gets you to heaven.*

Trials and Tribulations

All Souls, a staunch evangelical church, drew a sharp intake of breath when ASLAN began to work with homeless people who didn't live in the parish. Then, ASLAN began a partnership with a day centre run by a group of Roman Catholic nuns! You can imagine the depths of concern of many church members when they saw nearly 200 of their number getting involved as volunteers, many of them alongside people with whom there were enormous theological differences. Mike Fearon – who co-ordinated the five ASLAN teams working with the Roman Catholics – in spite of his impeccable evangelical credentials, found himself well and truly in the dog house!

The only theological confrontation to arise in eight years was with a lady RC volunteer who insisted on *telling* ASLAN members that *they* believed she was going to go to hell. Repeated assurances that they didn't think anything of the sort fell on fallow ground. The Catholic woman left convinced that these troublesome evangelicals held negative views about her dear faith that, in fact, they didn't hold at all! The lesson, of course, is: if you want to find out what someone else really believes, *ask them*, don't tell them. Chris Peacock reflects:

I believe that All Souls was not at all convinced that social action was a part of its ministry; their speciality was teaching and preaching. All too often, when Christians find any point of difference between themselves and their church leaders, they simply walk off and find themselves a new congregation. We should say to ourselves, 'God put me here for a reason, and maybe it was to be a lone voice in the wilderness of this place. Maybe it was to be unappreciated, and unloved, and unwanted, but I will stay here because God put me here and I will wait for him to tell me when it's time to move on.' I am by nature hot-headed and impatient, but God constrained me and kept me patient when I was passionate about the work and frustrated at how little support we seemed to be getting from All Souls Church.

I stayed at times when I was very frustrated and felt that I was banging my head against a brick wall – and I was able to stay and witness the way in which *the church lay leaders and ministers came around to endorse this work, to support this work, to own this work, and to be proud of this work.* That was God at work! We are all human, and we are all capable of being in error at times, but – when we are Christians – when a wrong path is taken, if you are genuine in your faith, God can gently guide us back to the path. All Souls continues to be a wonderful teaching and preaching church, so that bit of the ministry continues to grow and prosper, but now it is *also* one of the few London churches that is working with the homeless.

It took seven years, but God works at his own pace.

Christians who rightly have reputations for being truly godly are always more concerned about being godly than about preserving their reputations . . .

Welcome to the Banquet!

Chris Peacock eventually persuaded ASLAN to start a remarkable series of entertainment evenings, from a feeling that the people he was seeing at the day centre were being treated like cattle, queuing for food, with little time to talk at any length. 'What a life,' Chris felt:

When you're on the streets, you're ignored if you are lucky and abused if you are not. You go to a day centre, and you are one of hundreds queuing for charity. I wanted to open somewhere that people could receive more personal treatment, where there would be time to show some loving care. By giving them a printed invitation to produce for admission (which gave some control of numbers) we give them back a little respect, and let them feel a part of the real world again.

These innovative evenings cater for around two dozen clients, on alternate Saturday evenings, allowing for far greater personal contact – and growth – than with the tea run or day centre, each of which typically caters for 250 people each time. A sit-down meal is provided, with videos and other entertainments available.

I believe passionately in what Jesus asked us to do – to love the Lord and to love our fellow people. We were the first group in Britain to invite people to this sort of social event, and we sometimes get various sociologists and academics coming along to observe us. Time after time, these non-Christians have come up to me and said, 'There is an incredible atmosphere in this place. What is it?' And I have been able to reply, 'It is the presence of the Holy Spirit, because it sure ain't us!' People can sense God's presence for themselves, and he does double the work that a would-be orator standing up on his hind legs would ever do!

The next stage of innovation has been for ASLAN members to go to the homeless people, meeting them one-to-one to support, encourage and befriend them. 'I think it has been laid on enough hearts in ASLAN for me to believe it is God's will,' says Chris.

We may lay ourselves open to misunderstandings; these people we visit may come to see us as friends and expect to come to our houses. Since most of the clients are male, and most of the helpers are female, we need to be practical; something starting innocently could quickly become very nasty. But when a professional social worker visits someone at home, the client doesn't automatically assume that he or she has a right to visit the social worker at home.

To avoid any awkward misunderstandings, it is important to be quite clear about the professional nature of the relationship.

Taking the Lead

By nature, churches are usually cautious animals. To allow innovative and imaginative projects to develop and to begin the process of transformation, ordinary Christians usually need to strive to change the cautious mindset of their leadership, both on theological and practical concerns. The idea of going to church to get a nice warm glow is all very well, but the reality is often *a long series of frustrations*. The Christian consumerism culture needs to change if ordinary church members are to be effectively released for service. But what do you do about producing organisational change?

'The first thing is to build a vision for it,' says Doug Balfour, Tear Fund's General Director:

You will immediately be met with a whole load of assumptions that are not true; there will be a lot of baggage left over from the last time anybody did this. All the horror stories will come out. The only solution is patiently to work your way through all the objections and show how the project with which you want the church to be involved should be supported.

You need to explore the wider issues with the leaders: What's in it for us as a church? What are the benefits? Why should we be doing it in the first place? With most churches, it needs to be based on biblical understanding. Secondly, you need to take away the various obstacles that people put in the way of change. An effective way of building a vision is to take the leadership, the decision makers, to a place where something is actually happening on the ground, where they can get a picture of something they can emulate.

The church will probably need a change of emphasis, moving from being structural to being relational.

Being *relational* is not throwing away structure. It means taking the building blocks of structure and making them serve relationships. At Tear Fund, there is a set of teams run by team leaders that makes up our organisational structure. But those teams deliberately exist in the way they exist in order to release creativity; to create team work; and promote relational working between members and between teams.

Follow the Leader

There are many thwarted and frustrated people in churches across the world, but they often have only the most half-baked of ideas. These individuals sometimes need to go away and formulate *exactly what it is that they want to do*, and to put together a proper plan. The vision is built in stages. At first you need to formulate in your own mind a detailed concept; then you need to try to explore all the implications; next, get something down on paper that you can begin to share; research the idea and see what other people are doing elsewhere that is similar; revise and polish the idea; then present it to your church.

The church leaders may well send you off to do some more development work on the concept, and return with still more detail and, perhaps, some costing and budgets. Is it feasible? Will the leadership feel swamped by the imaginative idea? It's a gradual series of stages, but this *process* by which something is arrived at is usually the most important part so far as personal and community development is concerned.

Chris Peacock is keenly aware that training is an important aspect of starting any new venture. Any kind of children's work is particularly problematic:

> Working with children requires a huge amount of training, because of the legal requirements. With homeless people, there is no legal framework that demands training. I've never been convinced that there is much training required, short of giving people a few simple 'do's' and 'don'ts'. In a funny way, the more you train people, the more they *think* that they know how to handle every situation, the more vulnerable you make them. It's better to train people 'on the job'. A little humility goes a long way.

To bring a project to fruition requires someone to take responsibility for it. They must be prepared to invest as much time as required to develop it from the 'drawing board' to the actuality. But what are the qualities that such a project leader requires?

The leader needs to be someone whom the other people respect, but who will also stay in submission to the church leadership. Practical product management skills and/or a sense of vision are important, too. It needs to be someone with sensitivity to when people are getting upset, but who will also know when people desperately need some direction.

Could it be you?

Questions and exercises

- Can you think of a way you (and your family) can house yourself more economically? Look carefully at your answer. What is stopping you from putting the theory into practice?

- Make two lists, one of the factors that would make you a good leader, and the second list of factors that suggest this is not your forte. Get the friends who are praying for the vision with you to do the same. Discuss all the lists together, and decide who would make the best leader.
- Put together a detailed proposal of a scheme that your church (or a group of its members, or a group of churches) could run in your own locality. (Suggested headings: *Community, Needs, Church, Participation, Partnership, Resources, Timetable,* and *Cost*.) Spend time with God, praying and fasting over it.
- Discuss the detailed proposal with your church leadership, revising and developing it as necessary. Ask them to confirm the choice of leader arrived at above, or to appoint a leader of their own.
- If your church agrees to run the scheme under its umbrella, follow the *process* described in this book and begin to implement the scheme. If the church declines, continue working as a volunteer with someone else's scheme; and perhaps you could try to *transform* the church, with methods explained in the next chapter.

11

Make the Difference

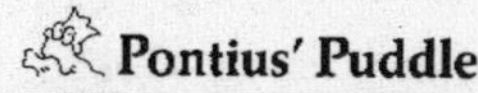

'The Truth is in here!' announced the handsome FBI agent, triumphantly holding up the leatherbound book with a cross prominently displayed on the front.

'In the Bible?' frowned his beautiful colleague, sceptically.

'Yes, Scully, it's definitely an "X" File; it says "X" on the cover. And it proves that history is a lie!'

'Agent Mulder, I've warned you about watching that rival TV show *Dark Skies* . . .' began Scully, but Mulder was determined to get to the end of his script:

'This book is the blueprint for the greatest conspiracy in world history. Two thousand years ago, God came down to be born as a hippie, and he went around preaching peace and love. After his abduction by a UFO – that's here in Acts 1:9 – his followers remained in contact with their leader using this ingenious and insidious technique called "prayer". They took his benign teaching – which addressed physical, mental and emotional, as well as spiritual needs – and set up a hive, called "The Church", to recruit many other people to the doctrine. They've got agents in every street. Some of them are little silver-haired ladies, while others are as young as five or six. There must be a billion of them out there somewhere,' said Mulder, the light casting playful shadows across his chiseled features. 'The British Prime Minister, and many of his cabinet, are part of the conspiracy.'

'That's incredible, Mulder,' said Scully, still sceptical. 'But what about little green men?'

'I don't know about extra-terrestrials, but these creatures called angels sound pretty interesting,' replied Mulder. Scully looked at him as though he was a couple of panes short of a greenhouse.

'It seems that the Church started out with a radical agenda,' Mulder continued. 'Recruitment went hand in hand with social care. It pioneered healthcare, racial equality, emancipation and tall steeples. The Church broke through the conspiracy of silence to call poverty and oppression by their true names. But it is now attempting to destabilise the global economy by distributing resources more fairly and evenly. Its participatory approach is growing very left-wing, and its development programme threatens our legal system by giving people free access to justice.'

'That's terrible. If justice comes into vogue, the FBI will be out of a job,' said Scully, crinkling her nose, just the way she did when she found something interesting during an autopsy.

'I know,' said Mulder. 'We'll just have to get by on our enormous salaries from this TV show.'

'But Mulder,' said Scully, beginning to smoulder seductively, 'that agenda doesn't sound like the churches that I know; they're all self-centred inward-looking cliques, with power in the hands of a few. They make the Republican party look democratic.'

'It's the most successful cover-up in history. It's so successful, most of the people in the Church have forgotten what they're supposed to be doing. Christians have become very good at stringing people along, making them think they want to produce real change in their lives, when – very often – all they want to do is to *talk about* change,' said Mulder, running his smooth hands lasciviously through his thick hair. 'They talk about love, but often they are too inhibited to demonstrate it . . .'

'Kiss me, Mulder!' demanded Scully.

'We don't do that sort of thing on this show,' he replied.

'Cut!' shouted the director.

Beyond the Pipedream

At this point, you too might feel like shouting 'Cut'. *It'll never happen in a month of Sundays!* you say. This radical option of personal participation by Christians in the development of their communities, may still seem to many people to be an unattainable pipedream. The world is filled with formulae for success in church growth, but a sacrificial ethos, denying self, has become a stranger in the list of contents from many discipleship courses. Though such criticism is frowned upon as tantamount to wife-beating, there seems to be an outbreak of tunnel vision in the church, as everything, seemingly, has to conform to a narrow range of pious activities and theoretical formulae that are at best ineffective, and at worst destructive and false.

'Theory without practice is not very good,' says Pastor Adrian Hawkes:

Somehow, theological colleges need to put the two together a lot more. When I first came out of college into full-time Christian work, in urban Middlesbrough, my constant thought was 'They never taught me this at Bible school!' There were such massive social problems, it was not unusual for a brick to come through the window when I was preaching! If we are to seek the Kingdom, intrinsically we must be involved with the current world and touching it where it really hurts.

People learn best, and change most, through 'doing things' and then reflecting on what they have just done. This reflection leads to further action. In order to make the most of the opportunities that the actions present us with, we have to have the ability to *think theologically*. Many Christians tend to view theology as a layer cake:

First you take the 'filling', the dogmatic theology, then you spread it inside the 'baked cake' or the practical assignment. The most important layer of the cake, however, is seen as the theology. But this is wrong! It perpetuates the myth that Christianity is just an intellectual theory. Theology is intensely *practical*, and unless it is taught on the street corner, in the pub, and in the cafés with ordinary people, we will rob God of the riches of our lives and potential.

Theology, far from being a layer cake, is like a *marble cake!* Action and reflection can happen simultaneously; they aren't always sequential. This is what makes true theology so gloriously messy! It simply will not conform to the models that many theological colleges impose upon it. Jesus himself would probably feel singularly uncomfortable in such surroundings if he were here in body today. Jesus actually experienced theoretical theological debate at the tender age of twelve (Luke 2:41ff.) and it didn't seem to impress him much. The way that he went about teaching his own followers was quite different, both in style and content, but also in the kind of people he chose as disciples in the first place!

There are many Christians who are perplexed or frustrated because they realise 'things are not as they should be'. Perhaps their theology is not sufficiently practical because they have never been taught how to think theologically in real-life situations.

Liberal theologian John Hick writes in his book *God Has Many Names*:

Dogmatic theology (which need not, however, be dogmatic in the sense of being assertive and unreasoning) studies and conserves the inherited tradition, having accepted its fundamental structure as permanently valid, because divinely revealed. Problematic theology, on the other hand, takes place at the interfaces between the tradition and the world – both the secular world and the wider religious world – and is concerned to create new solutions in the light of new situations . . . problematic theology sees its conclusion as hypothesis, open to revision and always seeking greater adequacy.

Some evangelical theologies – that have emerged from the poverty in the Third World (types of *problematic* theology) – perhaps create concerns and fears in the minds of those who fail to appreciate this distinct difference. *'Isn't a theology of the poor, poor theology?'* they wonder. This theological thinking explores how Christians can cope with the demands of a changing world. Good news to hapless people in broken communities, it explores how faith should be demonstrated through actions – it is the difference between *saying* the words 'I love you' and a kiss between lovers.

When will the Church stop fretting about the number of bottoms on seats, and focus on what is required to bring change to broken and damaged neighbourhoods? When the good news of the Gospel is translated into good news for communities – which it undoubtedly is – we will see churches full of people who have embarked on a journey of personal and community change! *The name of Jesus will be lifted up in worship by people who are discovering him in non-churchy jargon, and in ways which are relevant to their everyday existence.*

True Worship

Worship is telling God that you love him – and much more besides, *but saying it doesn't make it so.*

If the only time you ever saw your spouse was for an hour or so on a Sunday, when he or she came to visit you; but often didn't even take his or her coat off; sat in silence for most of the time; stood up to sing a few songs *at* you (sub-karaoke standard); listened to someone stand at the front and talk about you as though you weren't there, analysing what you used to do a few thousand years ago (!); read a few words of love at you out of a book; then studiously ignored you while standing around drinking coffee with some other people – *would you conclude from the experience that this person loved you?*

You'd be down to the marriage guidance counsellor like a shot! Yet this scenario takes place in many churches across the globe every Sunday. People *tell* God that they love him, but they don't *show* it. They don't 'walk it like they talk it'. They are 'stand-offish'. They treat God, at best, as though he were some demented patient in a sanatorium – and yet they claim to love him dearly! Let's face it, anyone who thinks such a coquettish display is an acceptable demonstration of love has got a couple of wheels missing from their bicycle!

If you love someone, then you:

- Spend time talking with them (not *at* them).
- Listen attentively to them.
- Try to make yourself the kind of person that they want you to be.
- Share in their interests.
- Rejoice in your shared values.
- Enjoy intimacy.
- Go places together.
- Enjoy sharing in activities together.

God is not really the sort who goes out 'clubbing' very much; but neither does he like to stay at home with his pipe and slippers. This dynamic deity likes to be in the thick of the action where there is poverty or suffering. He gets his hands dirty by getting involved in people's lives. He is the good neighbour who can always be counted upon to babysit, to help with the old folk, to comfort the bereaved; to nurse the sick, feed the hungry, heal the brokenhearted, and transform the community.

If you don't care for those sorts of things, then you and God are not going to get along too well in your relationship unless you begin to make a few changes in your own life! *Many Christians who wonder why their spiritual lives are so drab feel that way because they are just 'not in the same place' as God; they are separated by different agendas and conflicting values.*

A Lack of Fresh Air?

We have now covered a lot of ground in this book and *you* may be thinking: 'It's all very well all this stuff about Christian community transformation, the role of the local church and everything, but it doesn't take into account *my* circumstances. It doesn't reflect the situation in *my* church.' As Jesus's original disciples observed, 'This teaching is too hard.'

David Evans had a conversation with a church minister who assured him: 'There is no way members of my congregation could take on any responsibility for more action in the community or anywhere else.' Was this indicative of leadership which was 'controlling' rather than 'releasing'? For those of us who are leaders, to change our understanding of our own roles in leadership is difficult. It will mean letting go of much of the familiar types of activity and thinking and then embracing the new. A failure to change could spell death in the longer term for the church – and probably for the minister in the shorter term, if he (or she) isn't given a break!

Currently, so much of Christian living is *theoretical*, bearing little resemblance to the model of church suggested in much of the New Testament. Our church sub-culture sometimes seems bent on minimising freedom to do anything in the name of the church or the Lord. If churches are so estranged from their communities, perhaps that explains why so many evangelistic activities are so ineffectual – they answer the questions that no one is asking!

This bizarre church sub-culture is endlessly fascinating. Most people know exactly what to do; they've done it every week since they first arrived, and they have long since 'learned the ropes'. They know what posture to be in when the prayers are said, and how to look interested during the sermon. But observe the tangible embarrassment in some churches when children are allowed to wander. Observe what happens when a stranger with problems in his or her life comes in, who is not from a churchy background and who doesn't know the 'etiquette'. Will he or she feel at ease, and be able to discuss matters with a sympathetic listener? *Will pigs fly?* No, the sub-culture often suffocates innovation and new approaches to the perennial issues and problems which continue to beset many congregations.

The lack of depth in some charismatic churches is leaving many believers feeling alienated and divorced from the expressions of the body of Christ as we have it today. The move of the Spirit that swept through churches across the globe around 1994 launched a thousand ministries and led many to believe that revival was close at hand. Certainly, many congregations and individual Christians have been genuinely refreshed by the so-called Toronto Blessing.

Mike Fearon's analysis of the phenomenon, *A Breath of Fresh Air*, suggested that those who have been specially touched by God need to find their place in the mission field, where they can truly begin to serve God: 'The Spirit's outpouring is for people to receive and to take away to their own church and their own community – it's wrong to keep coming back. It's not for them to keep, it's for them to give away. You're shopping in a religious supermarket, when you should be serving in a spiritual soup kitchen!' Christian community development is surely the 'spiritual soup kitchen' of the twenty-first century, where the needs of a wounded world can receive attention.

Roger Forster, leader of Ichthus Christian Fellowship, in spite of a rich blessing with the gifts of the Spirit, said: 'We are maintaining a church programme that contains a lot of political and social action. A couple of our leading lights employ twenty-four people on a lifeskills course for people out of work. They were a couple of the first to get blessed and to return with great zeal to their work!' Steve Chalke has said that charismatic blessing 'is only good if it equips people to move out into society. We need to get out into the world to be salt and light. We must be committed to seeing a world that can laugh and rejoice.' For theological college principal Graham Cray, 'Stickability in the most hopeless of situations is the fruit of the anointing of the Spirit. We are given security by the Spirit that we can be in there feeling the pain, but without becoming bereft of hope.'

A Vision of Transformation

The first phase of setting about changing things is essentially an internal cost-counting exercise for your church. It aims to unite the church's perceptions of its role with expectations of what is possible. This first stage takes a long hard look at the *objections* people raise to getting involved at all in seeking to be transforming influences in the community. Some of the answers are radical, but all the solutions are realistic. This process also uncovers the assumptions and values which underpin *what* we do, and *how* we do it, in our local fellowships. (You may need to bring in an outside facilitator to help you with this.)

Most churches do certain things in certain ways, and the way they do it betrays the values to which they hold. At one church meeting, a congregation was asked to put away the chairs and stand in the middle of the room. On one wall was a large sign saying 'agree' and on the opposite wall a corresponding sign saying 'disagree'. A series of statements were read out and each person was asked to position him- or herself on a line between the two signs, according to how much they agreed or disagreed with the statements. After a few innocuous ice-breakers – 'Leyton Orient will win the FA cup', 'Bart Simpson is well behaved' – several statements were read out which related to the church's avowed mission and role within the community.

The action of moving about the room helped the congregation to reflect, and many individuals positioned themselves in ways quite contrary to the church's agreed policies. They had never actually agreed with the policies, but had never really reflected upon them properly either – until now, as a result of physically 'doing something'. Now the church knew – quite literally! – where people really *stood*, and could begin to address the problems. The results were stunningly – and disturbingly – different from anything people would have said if they had been sitting around a table 'being polite'.

Tithes of Time

David Evans remembers facilitating an event at a typical local church. The various members of the congregation who were present called out all the different activities that the church did. Since it was a fairly traditional evangelical church, David fully expected 'evangelism' to be near the top of the activities listed. It didn't appear however. The people listed about twenty different areas of work that the church did, but still no 'evangelism' was mentioned. Eventually, after the list seemed to be getting exhausted, he said that it was interesting that evangelism hadn't been mentioned . . .

There was an embarrassed pause, and one or two people cleared their throats. David probed a little more and discovered that the people weren't at all convinced that this activity actually worked! Most people there agreed that the usual methods of evangelism left them feeling embarrassed and self-conscious. Introducing conversations about the Gospel, in terms which are foreign to most members of the public, felt forced and were met with a degree of hostility which stopped progress in its tracks . . .

What are the assumptions which that church carried around in their minds about how evangelism should be done? What were the barriers to be overcome in thinking about evangelism in different terms? In answering these questions through collective discussion, a church could begin to build its *own agenda for change*. The incident highlighted how easily churches slip into ways of doing things which, unless critically reviewed, quickly become out-moded and irrelevant. Sharing the good news of Christ will never become irrelevant, indeed such is its importance that the Church has to keep listening to God and the world and find effective ways of communicating with ordinary people.

If people feel they have no further time to give to *another* 'church thing', then ask people what they give their time and energy to currently. If it's lots of church meetings, could the congregation corporately decide to reduce the number of meetings to release people into areas of work they feel passionate about? If it's work in the community of different types, could work be taken on by the church in a way that supports and builds on *existing* commitments of individual members? (For example, if one church member helps to take handicapped children on holidays, could other members with similar concerns join in and support this activity?)

In a pleasant rural church, the congregation was led in a participatory manner to discover what people in the church most enjoyed spending their time doing; what their passions and convictions were. After ninety minutes, pieces of paper around the room painted a map of activities carried out by church members. Beforehand, many members of the congregation had considered that many of the good works they carried out were done *by them as individuals*; now they came to see an elaborate tapestry of interlaced activity, with mutual concerns *shared with people* they had hitherto never realised were active partners in the same areas of concern. *Networks were strengthened as a result of this participatory reflection; the church began to own and to help with activities its members had previously carried out on their own; and individuals were encouraged and strengthened through the feeling that the church valued and affirmed the work they did.*

Although the ideas explored in this book are exciting and innovative (participation by Christians in the community, and the church welcoming participation by the community in church activity) there is a need to be aware of and anticipate the *problems* that may follow. These obstacles will be both practical and theological. Churches need to be in the process of sorting these out as they commence, rather than 'coming a cropper' once they are under way!

A Handful of Change

The second stage is to try new approaches, being trained up in them and starting to handle them confidently. Our experience has been that when people are trained in these practical ways of assessing needs, the trainees in the churches get very eager and excited – it really has been quite amazing!

Drawing a handful of young people into dialogue about real-life issues proved to be so rewarding in one group that, very quickly, a church congregation who had been used to trying all sorts of evangelistic events heard very clearly what the young people outside the church really found to be a 'turn off' and what was 'cool'. Having a lesson in what makes for effective approaches to evangelism from non-church youth groups is 'different' if nothing else!

In another church where training has been carried out, the congregation undertook an exercise in *historical mapping*. As a group, they drew a line on a long horizontal piece of paper, and put dates on it going back as far as the oldest member of the group could remember. They then marked on the line all the events which had happened in the community, or which had affected it. Good aspects of events were marked above the line, bad things or aspects of events, below it. Some remembered the Second World War – what were the negative things about that time? What were the positive things for the community?

They went on to note the building of the high-rise blocks of flats – so good when they first were built, but now so awful – and they discussed reasons for the change. Issues were discussed that had never been brought up before. The group remarked on the episode of the infamous gas tank that a big corporation had tried to situate in the middle of the town, and how the whole community had come together to fight against the move! They remembered the sense of victory when the community succeeded in convincing the company that they should put it elsewhere.

In raising such memories, the people in the church realised there was tremendous potential for working with the local community, being catalytic in making sure that the issues which are thrust on to a community by all sorts of influences are met by just and godly responses. The idea is for local churches to be involved in finding good solutions, and then to provide a focus for celebration and reflection on what happens.

The *strength* of these approaches is also that they are completely unthreatening to people outside the church – there is no sense of a pre-formed 'church agenda' which seeks to 'force the beliefs of the church down our throats', as is commonly felt by non-believers.

Belief, hope, change and transformation come all right – but in the altogether more subversive way of yeast leavening bread, or mustard seeds sprouting into enormous trees, to use two of Jesus's favourite metaphors! In all this, there will undoubtedly be need for more overt evangelism – but this will be done in the context of culturally-relevant church services where non-believers expect to hear such things, and in which they will be far more willing to listen, given the unconditional support and hard work going on beyond the church walls!

A Month of Sundays

One of the surprising reflections on this whole process is the realisation of just how *non*-participative church life is! So much energy and goodwill can be generated within congregations, when people are given a voice. To make it happen constructively, congregations and fellowships need to have agreed the basic values which underpin their life together. Participative methods can be used to set objectives, and to prioritise activities within a church, as well as elsewhere. In particular, there is a need for *a changed set of expectations* with regard to the role of ministers and leaders.

In summary and conclusion, what has preceded this chapter is a description of a new culture of church and 'care-evangelism'. We have said that not only do churches need to be outward-looking, but that we need to *encourage non-believers to take part in 'good works'* as a means to help *explain and reflect upon* a Christian world view, and the importance of Christ.

This reflection happens when Christians are working alongside people in *partnership*, in a shared task. It demands that Christians in these situations have a coherent and natural way of talking about their faith on a one-to-one basis. It means that we *intentionally* and *deliberately* grasp opportunities to help people put things together in their minds.

It'll never happen in a month of Sundays?

'In a month of Sundays' is exactly when the Church *will* be transformed! When every day of the month is treated like a Sunday by Christians whose daily lives are wholly dedicated to a holy God, and their vision is fired up with a desire to truly become their brother's keeper – a good neighbour to all in the community. Start treating everyone as though they were a member of your immediate family, and the world will begin to change around you.

Remember that you can't do everything on your own. Sound partnerships are the secret of success in community development. Along with the *participation* of the people whose lifestyle you are seeking to help improve and judicious use of the action-reflection approach, real headway can be made in building God's Kingdom.

The Church's mission is *not* to be like a pair of scissors, evangelism and social care acting together. It should be like a keenly-whetted *scalpel blade* – with outreach and social action the two sides of the blade; you can't have one without the other, any more than you can have a one-sided sheet of paper! The process of mission should utilise activities which are *simultaneously* caring and evangelistic. This Scalpel of Mission must cut smoothly and cleanly to the cancers and tumours that plague our world – slicing away at emotional, mental and physical entanglements as well as the spiritual.

We began with C. S. Lewis's junior demon Wormwood exhorting you not to read this book, but to have an easy life instead. What do you suppose Wormwood's uncle, Screwtape, might be writing to his junior colleague about *you* at this very moment? Perhaps this is what Wormwood has just found in his e-mail:

The Screwtape E-mail

My dear Wormwood,

All is lost! How can you ever have been so foolish as to allow this person to have read the whole way through a book as dangerous as *From Strangers to Neighbours?* It's 4-X rated! And have I not expressly told you to allow Christians to have access to no literature stronger than *Trainspotters' Weekly* and *Churchmouse Gazette?*

I'm not a happy little demon, Wormwood. Your carelessness has allowed harmless Christians to start getting ideas into their heads about effective evangelism. So long as they sat in neat rows in church, where they could pose no danger – and while they foolishly expected people to come to them and hear someone lecture at them from the front every Sunday – they hadn't a hope in Heaven of recruiting new members. As long as they continued to believe that Christian community development was boring and 'unsexy' – shrouded in incomprehensible sociological jargon – they were content merely to wear out their church furniture with their bottoms. *Now they know how many beans make five!*

Just look what you've gone and allowed to happen! They've found out all about participatory leadership, the value of partnerships, and the biblical perspectives on wealth, employment and homelessness! They've stopped thinking that action-reflection is boring. They used to believe anyone suggesting that good theology could be moulded in pastoral situations, instead of in a theological college, was a couple of drawers short of a dresser, but now they'll *all* be doing it! Most terrible of all, they've discovered that the Bible actually has a powerful statement to make – not just about religion, but on social, political and economic issues as well. *They'll all be turning into evangelicals if you don't watch out!*

You're playing with fire, Wormwood! While these daft Christians were too clappy-happy for their faith to make any impact upon the communities in which they live, they were no threat to Our Father Below. So long as they did no more than drop a few coins in a collection tin from a misplaced sense of guilt, they were harmless enough creatures. Now, if your Christians begin to step out in faith and make contact with others who will join in transforming their community, they may find out how important they all really are in God's Kingdom. They might start to acquire *confidence* in their faith, they'll begin to feel a sense of *belonging* and – worst of all – they might finally discover that the Enemy has a purpose and direction for their lives!

If that wasn't bad enough, those interfering busybodies, David Evans and Mike Fearon, have also gone and told everybody the truth about world mission! While Westerners thought that people in the Third World were ignorant savages in need of handouts, their colonial instincts prevented them from realising how much they could *learn* from their overseas brothers and sisters. Now these discriminatory and bigoted attitudes are beginning to change, we have a major problem on our hands. We really can't have Christians dealing fairly and justly with one another – linking hands in fellowship and partnership across the globe. The very idea makes me feel quite ill!

You have only one hope, my dear incompetent Wormwood. The book has now been read, but you must *under no circumstances allow the reader to put its methods into practice!* We've done a very good job, up to now, of making Christians believe that social action was a ruse devised by Our Father Below to divert them from their endless string of tedious meetings; but now this wretched book has blown our cover! Be a bad little demon, and make sure the reader is distracted by an immediate need for personal gratification – a TV programme, a bit of sex, a cup of coffee or a cosy chat with a friend – anything will do, so long as you can get the reader to put down the book and never think about its contents ever again.

Why, if these Christians begin to believe that they can make a real difference, they will start to take positive action, and then they will soon discover that *helping people to improve their lives is often fun and enjoyable*; once the ol' feelgood factor begins to kick in, there will be no stopping them!

Their neighbours will begin to walk around with smiles on their faces, in place of their usual gloomy frowns; they may even start talking to one another! Once they realise that local Christians have – some of them for the first time in their lives – done something beneficial *with* (not *for*) them, they may begin the process of reflection. Hades forbid! Some of them may become interested in the Christian faith and, before you know it, we'll have a streetful of new Christian converts on our hands!

Now then, Wormwood you clumsy wretch, there are five things that I expressly forbid you to allow any Christian reader to do:

- Don't let them **pray** about this! Once they've got their head office behind them, we'll never get them back again into their usual pious but ineffectual glow.
- Never let them **promote** this book's contents to a single living soul; we've got to keep all these ideas strictly quarantined or we'll have a major outbreak of happy communities, filled with freedom, justice, mercy and all the other nauseous stuff.
- Don't let them make any changes to **simplify** their own lifestyle. So long as they keep buying things they don't really need (and can't really afford) they'll be surrounded with far more clothes, furniture, CDs, deodorants, computer games, videos, futons and fondue sets than they can possibly use – and that will give them more scope to use their time unwisely.
- Keep them from thinking too deeply. Once they fully **reflect** on all these concepts, they'll start to become active members of the community, then there'll be Heaven to pay!
- Do not let them write, phone or e-mail any of the resource providers and development agencies listed in the next few pages. If they realise that they can get free information that will **help** them to find their role in Christian mission – just by sending an e-mail to Tear Fund's UK Action [ukaction@tearfund.dircon. co.uk] – then we'll both be out of work!

Now, my dear inept Wormwood, see to it that Christians and their churches make no changes whatsoever to their usual apathetic state!

Yours very angrily, *and ravenously hungry,*

Screwtape
Archdemon

Epilogue

The young barrister approached Jesus with a superior disposition. Apparently, he had conceived of the perfect line of questioning to undermine the Galilean peasant. So what, he wondered was the qualification for eternal life? (Lk. 10:25). It turned out to be a rhetorical question based on familiar Old Testament law, and so he presented a supplementary question: 'And who' he asked, 'is my neighbour?' Bible scholars and preachers since that time have been grateful for the story of the Good Samaritan which flowed from that question, but it is unlikely that the young barrister was very pleased with his public performance.

It is likely too that in the society of Jesus's time few of the bystanders would have been very comfortable overhearing this battle of wit and wisdom. It would have been too close for comfort. Essentially it was the difference between what we know and what we do about what we know.

What makes it worse is that Scripture brings many witnesses against us. The Old Testament code in general, and the eighth century B.C. prophets in particular, show only too clearly that belief and behaviour go hand in hand. Whatever religion is about, true faith in God compels us to do justice, love mercy and walk self-effacingly with God (Micah 6:8). As far as Jesus was concerned then, the summary of the Law at its pristine best is to love God and our neighbour with everything we have. In a word, strangers become neighbours.

Not even grace it seems saves us from this imperative. Credible Christianity means that belief and behaviour are two sides of the same coin. Indeed, grace insists on it, and the moral imperative of love is the genius of the relationship between Matthew 24 and 25.

Here, the great apocalyptic symbolism of Matthew 24 is unashamedly and uncomfortably related to our practical responses to the hungry, thirsty prisoner.

From Strangers to Neighbours has taken us through this imperative of transformational love and involvement. While it chided us for non- and inappropriate involvement it has presented us with an exhaustive catalogue of good models for transformation. It is the product of numerous reflections from the practitioners of love who experiment with the tools for change on behalf of the poor, disenfranchised and marginalised. Undoubtedly, it expresses frustration with the snail-pace application of biblical propositions in the interest of those we claim to love. It is committed to converting strangers into the people next door.

Jesus's punchline must have stayed with the professional believer for some time. I hope it did not immobilise him. Jesus said something like: 'Now that we have had this discussion, you go and do it.' Maybe those on the edge of the crowd pretended that they couldn't quite hear.

Joel Edwards

Addresses

Tear Fund's UK Action

UK Action
Tear Fund
100 Church Road
Teddington
Middlesex
TW11 8QE
Tel: Tear Fund Enquiry Team 0181 943 7864/5

The Evangelical Alliance

Evangelical Alliance
Whitefield House
186 Kennington Park Road
London
SE11 4BT
Tel: 0171 582 0228

The Evangelical Alliance can put you in touch with many organisations working in almost every area of community-transforming work. Many of these organisations produce excellent resources which readers may find helpful.

Christian Action Networks

Christian Action Networks (CANs) operate in many of the UK's larger cities. They aim to network projects, churches and organisations to ensure that the impact of work being carried out by evangelical Christians is maximised. The EA can put you in touch with your local CAN co-ordinator.

Resources

The UK Action Toolkit

The Toolkit is a pioneering training resource combining biblical reflection, practical exercises and advice to help churches think through the issues of getting involved in their community.

If you would like further details, please contact UK Action at the above address or e-mail UK Action on: ukaction@tearfund.dircon. co.uk

Faces of Poverty

A sixteen-page A4 booklet packed with background information on UK poverty, case studies of churches making a difference locally and the UK Action programme. Available from Tear Fund.

Neighbours Pack

A twenty-four-page folder designed to help churches understand UK poverty. Fact Sheets on health, drugs, young people, cities, unemployment and housing, prayers, talks, songs, ideas for action are all included in the pack. Available from Tear Fund.

Bibliography

Andrews, D. *Can You Hear the Heartbeat?* (Hodder and Stoughton:1989)

Baldwin, D. *Open Doors, Open Minds* (Highland:1994)

Barley, G. and Fearon, M. *The Long Way Home* (Kingsway:1996)

Beckett, F. *Called to Action* (Fount:1989)

Chalke, S. *I Believe in Taking Action* (Hodder and Stoughton:1996)

Chambers, R. *Rural Development* (Longman:1983)

Chester, T. *Awakening to a World of Need* (IVP:1993)

De Carvalho, S. *The Street Children of Brazil* (Hodder and Stoughton:1996)

Dixon, P. *Out of the Ghetto and Into the City* (Nelson Word/Pioneer:1995)

Fearon, M. *A Breath of Fresh Air* (Eagle:1994)

Fearon, M. *No Place Like Home* (Triangle:1989)

Grigg, V. *Companion to the Poor* (Albatross:1984)

Hick, J. *God Has Many Names* (Macmillan:1980)

Holman, B. *FARE Dealing* (Community Development Foundation:1997)

Homan, M. *Promoting Community Change* (Brooke/Cole Pub. Co.:1993)

Hope, A, and Trimmel, S. *Training for Transformation* (Mambo Press:1984)

Kraybill, D. *The Upside-down Kingdom* (Marshalls:1978)

Mangalwadi, V. *Truth and Social Reform* (Spire:1989)

Marchant, C. *Signs in the City* (Hodder and Stoughton:1985)

Marris, P. *Meaning and Action* (Routledge and Kegan Paul:1982)

McCloughry, R. *Belief in Politics* (Hodder and Stoughton:1996)

Morisy, A. *Beyond the Good Samaritan* (Mowbray:1997)

Ronnby, A. *Mobilising Local Communities* (Avebury:1995)
Smith, G. *Poverty and its Alleviation* (University of Bradford:1992)
Smith, G. *Biblical Bases of Socio-Political Action* (unpublished)
Sider, R. *Rich Christians in an Age of Hunger* (Hodder and Stoughton:1990)
Sider, R. *Evangelism and Social Action* (Hodder and Stoughton:1993)
Sine, T. *The Mustard Seed Conspiracy* (MARC Europe:1984)
Taylor, M. *Signposts to Community Development* (Community Development Foundation:1992)
Tear Fund. *The Debt Cutter's Handbook* (Jubilee 2000:1996)
Tear Fund. *Give It Back Worship and Action Guide* (Tear Fund:1996)
Tondeur, K. *Say Goodbye to Debt* (Marshall Pickering:1994)
Wallis, J. *The New Radical* (Lion:1983)